Standing on His Promises

Finding Comfort, Hope, and Purpose in the Midst of Your Storm

To Betty
love and blessings
Joan M Blake
3/28/09

Joan M. Blake

Key to Life Publishing Company
P.O. Box 190971, Boston, MA 02119

Standing on His Promises:
Finding Comfort, Hope, and Purpose in the Midst of Your Storm
ISBN 978-0-9814609-0-1
ISBN 978-0-9814609-1-8 (pbk)

Published by: Key to Life Publishing Company
P.O. Box 190971
Boston MA 02119

Contents

Contents

Preface

In every life there are times of joy and times of crisis. During times of crisis, we face emotional issues and other stumbling blocks that inhibit our growth, hold us captive, and keep us from walking in our destiny and achieving our purposes, purposes that God set for us before the foundation of the world. Such stumbling blocks might include family issues, job issues, or church issues. The list can go on.

Standing on His Promises: Finding Comfort, Hope, and Purpose in the Midst of Your Storm, was born out of joyous and painful times that I experienced while living in Trinidad, leaving Trinidad, my birthplace, to come to America, meeting the challenges of college, and being a wife and mother. I sought God and He gave me strength, comfort, hope, and purpose during my darkest hours. I honor, praise, and thank Him for the wisdom and insights that He imparted to me throughout the course of writing and revising this book, without which, this book could not be possible.

This book is written for women of all ages, nationalities, colors, cultures, religions, for stay-at-home moms, women in positions of power, business owners, students, single parents, single women, pastors, evangelists, lay leaders, women and men from all walks of life.

The purpose of this book is to give women and men encouragement and hope in their everyday lives, to enable them to trust and rest in God and to experience peace and joy regardless of the situations they face. Peace and rest come when one makes a conscious decision to surrender all of life's challenges and fears to God, to draw near to Him in prayer and praise, and to thank Him continually for His mighty acts. God loves and cares for you. Most importantly, God is sovereign, and He knows and controls every situation you face, from its inception. With tender hands, He is carrying you through your difficulty; with His grace, He is giving you the power to face and to overcome your challenges and fears and to press on toward your destiny. God promises never to leave or forsake you (Josh.1:5).

I have dedicated this book to my entire family: my husband, Carl, my sons, Tony and Rese, and my daughters, Monique and Jo-An. My family has been an immense blessing to me.

I thank my husband, Carl, for his love, for continually standing with me, for encouraging me, and for making it possible for me to achieve my goals, even when it meant his sacrificing vacation time, and also for doing considerably more to keep our family together.

Tony has been a great listener and encourager. As a husband and father, he demonstrates virtues of love, patience, kindness, gentleness, and compassion in his family as well as in ours. I am grateful to God for him.

Rese has shown love, support, encouragement, and compassion for his sister Jo-An. His compassion extends to those who are disadvantaged. I thank Rese for his willingness to share with others how God has restored his life.

Monique has been a joy to my life. I thank God for birthing patience in her, for the unique gifts with which He has blessed her, and for how she has used these gifts for His glory. I am grateful for her love, comfort, continual feedback, support, and friendship over the years. She has also been a moral support to her sister Jo-An.

Jo-An has been God's gift to me, a testing ground to help me understand what God's unconditional love is, to show me that God is no respecter of persons, and that He loves Jo-An just as much as He loves me or anyone else. My experience with Jo-An has helped me understand what patience is and how God has been patient with me. God has helped me live a life of faith in the midst of pain, and proves to me what He can do in the life of an individual when I show the same level of unconditional love to another human being, that He has shown to me.

Thanks go to Ruth Robinson and Cherry Gorton for their support during the copyedit stages of the book, to Anika Thomas who supplied me with additional information on the foods and juices of Trinidad and Tobago, to Renee Bergeron for designing the cover and formatting the book, and to the many friends and family members who have supported and encouraged me.

Because of the personal nature of this book, I have decided to comply with my family's wishes to use middle names for our daughters and nicknames for our sons in order to protect their identities. In Chapter Sixteen, "Experiencing Fear of Fear," and elsewhere in the book, I have used fictitious names to protect the reputations of the individuals of the bed and breakfast and others.

I pray that, as you read this book, God will pour out so many blessings on you that you will not have room to receive them. I pray that you will be free from the stains of your past and from current situations that hold you hostage, and that you will walk as a woman or man of God, renewed in your mind and set free by the blood of the Lamb.

1

Living in Trinidad

I was born on the island of Trinidad and Tobago, a small island in the West Indies, South of Venezuela. My father, John, and my mother, Agnes, had six of us: five daughters and one son, plus two older brothers on my mom's side from a previous marriage. I had no idea that my life would change to the point that everyone in the family would look to me for guidance. We were an average, working family, not having much but looking eagerly to receive life's unexpected blessings.

Of the country's 1.3 million inhabitants (as of 2005), most (96%) reside on the island of Trinidad and the remaining (4%) in Tobago. The island of Trinidad and Tobago consists of various ethnic groups: East Indians (originally from Northern India) represent about 40.3%, blacks 39.5%, mixed races 18.4%, whites .6%, Chinese and other 1.2%.[1] The religions are as follows: 26% are Roman Catholics; 22% are Hindus; 8% are Anglicans; 5% are Muslims; and 4% are Seventh-day Adventists. Other faiths account for the remaining thirty-five percent.[2] The official language of the island is English. Colloquial language spoken is reflective of Trinidad and Tobago's European and African heritage. Other languages include Hindi, French-Creole, and Spanish.[3]

The island's economy is dependent on tourism and natural gas but it also supplies food and beverages as well as cement to the Caribbean region.[4]

Trinidad and Tobago covers an area of 1,979 square miles,[5] with hills and mountains in plain view. It is surrounded by water, scenic beaches, and palm trees, which invite relaxation for tourists and residents alike. It is home to cricket tournaments and carnival celebrations. The residents of the island stage a pre-Lenten carnival, a two-day celebration on the streets of Port-of-Spain, in early February of each year. People dress in various costumes and display floats of all kinds that they have made themselves over the past year. Calypso singers and children's carnival contests precede the actual carnival celebrations.

The island's landscape is covered with naturally grown, perennial tropical plants with flowers of various shades of pink, yellow, orange, red, and green, pleasing to the eye. There are also fruit trees, which include mango, plum, chenet, tamarind, citrus, papaya, peewah, pineapple, pomerac, pommecythere, sapodilla, soursop, bananas, plantain, passion fruit, coconut, avocado, barbadeen, and guava. Vegetable gardens grow an assortment of vegetables such as corn, tomatoes, cabbages, cucumbers, bodi, ochroes, lettuce, patchoi, sweet peppers, celery, cauliflower, sorrel, breadfruit, and pumpkin; and root vegetables such as dasheen, cassava, edoes, yam, tania, and sweet potatoes.

An array of delicacies and juices are made from the fruits, for example, curried mango chutney dish and stewed and red mango are made from the mango fruit; jelly, jam, and cheese are made from the guava fruit;

and juices are made from mango, coconut, guava, papaya, passion fruit, and pineapple.

Main dishes include callaloo, coo-coo, pelau, rice and peas, cornmeal dumplings, roti, fried or stewed fish (king fish, red fish, shark, and others), chicken, duck, turkey, fried and roast bakes, buljol, accra, and boiled or fried plantain.

Callaloo is made from dasheen leaf or spinach, is cooked and blended with ochroes and seasonings into a thick, smooth, dark-green paste, lightly salted, rich in aroma and appetizing. It is occasionally cooked with crab meat. Coo-coo made with cornmeal, ochroes, coconut milk, butter, salt, and pepper is pale-yellow, mushy, and has a mild taste. Pelau is rice cooked with pigeon peas (dried green peas), seasonings, chopped chicken or beef and coconut milk, while rice and peas dish is prepared without meat. Burned sugar colors the rice, peas, and the meat giving them a dark-brown appearance. The rice and peas are firmly cooked; herbal and other seasonings create a Mediterranean aroma and delicious taste. Cornmeal dumplings are firm and pale-yellow. The dough is cut into small shapes to make small dumplings for soups or larger shapes for a meal of dumplings and cod fish. Roti, an Indian dish, is a thin flour wrap that is prepared in different ways: as a dhalpurie roti made with split peas, saffron and other ingredients or as a plain roti or buss-up-shut, which is broken up into sections. The roti wraps are soft, off-white in color, lightly salted, and filled with curried and seasoned chicken, beef, goat or vegetables. The yellow fillings are juicy, mouth-watering, hot, and flavorsome. Buljol is made from dried codfish which is washed and stripped and mixed with oil, onions, tomatoes, garlic, sweet peppers or pimentos. The dish is oily, lightly salted, spicy, soft, and tasty. Accra is also made from dried codfish, but is put into a batter of flour with seasonings and cooked in oil. Accra is a spicy fish dish that is lightly salted, crunchy, greasy, but delicious. Fried and roast bakes are formed from the dough that is prepared with baking powder and are cooked until they become light brown; dough is fried in oil to make crispy fried bakes and baked to make moist roasted bakes. A fried bake resembles a bun and a roast bake resembles a large pizza without the toppings. All meats and fish are highly seasoned with herbs that leave a fresh aroma and mouth-watering taste. Boiled or fried plantains resemble bananas but are longer; they are yellow, soft when cooked or fried, and compliment main dishes.

Holiday favorites include sweetbread, black cake, ginger beer, sorrel, mauby, and ponche de crème. Sweetbread is made with flour, grated coconut, mixed fruit, spices, margarine, raisins, currants, milk, vanilla essence, baking powder, and sugar and cooked until it is slightly brown; it has a sweet taste and the spices give it a wonderful aroma. Black cake is made with flour, eggs, butter, sugar, spices and rum or wine, lime peel, vanilla essence, cinnamon, and baking powder; and with raisins, currants, prunes, and cherries grinded together. The browning liquid made from sugar colors the cake black, and the ingredients and spices create a sweet, rich, moist, and delicious taste. Ginger beer is made from grated ginger and other spices which give it a light yellow appearance and leaves a burning sensation in one's mouth. Sorrel, which is a deep-red, sweetened, but a slightly sour drink, is made from a flower that is dried after its seeds are removed and boiled with certain spices. Mauby drink, pale brown in color, mild and bitter-sweet is made from the bark from a tree which is boiled with spices. Ponche de crème made with eggs, milk, rum, lime, angostura bitters, and other flavorings, is a thick, creamy, drink similar to eggnog but with a fruity flavor.

The climate of Trinidad is usually hot and sunny, about 89 degrees, with the exception of intermittent rainy periods between June and December. The heat mixed with gusts of wind sweep through the air making one feel joyful and rejuvenated. People use umbrellas to ward off the sun and dress casually in short-sleeved shirts, dresses, skirts, pants, and shorts.

I lived in the village of Morvant, situated outside Port-of-Spain. Throughout the day, one could hear a mother calling for her children to do chores and the children, engulfed in their play of jump rope or cricket, pretending not to hear her beckoning calls.

The neighbors were poor or working class people who reached out to each other. There was never a day that Miss Peterson didn't say, "Good morning, Mrs. Moses. How'd you do?"

My mother's reply would always be, "I am so-so yes, darling." On many occasions, my mother would talk to a neighbor near the fence while hanging out her clothes to dry, or someone would drop by our home and say to my dad, "How'd you do, ole mann?" My dad would play a game of chess with his guest, and before the evening ended, there would be several people playing chess, or "draft," as we called it. A neighbor might visit because she needed flour, some tea leaves to make tea for her children, or an onion to season her meat, and my mother always provided her with what she needed.

When I was a young child, my mother and father always wanted me to confess which of them, was my favorite parent. I never admitted that my father was my favorite for fear that my mother might become jealous, but my mother knew. I loved my father more because he appeared calmer than my mother, and I could get a word through to him. My mother was boisterous, and, although she worked hard at home and was kind and caring to us her children, she never took time to get to know us. It was work and more work for her. From a young age, I knew what I wanted. I was very independent and opinionated but also obedient to my parents, knowing that was the better way to go. I tended to spiritual matters like church and was careful to excel in school. I wanted to please my parents and to get their affirmation. Being their first daughter, I felt I had a responsibility to be all that they wanted me to be.

The first important day in my life was my First Communion, which I took when I was eight years old. Although I wasn't sure what it all meant, I knew it was a happy, momentous occasion, one that would change my life forever as I learned to love God, obey His commandments, and live a life worthy of Him. I wore a white nylon gown, a veil, and a crown, and, with hands clasped, received Holy Communion for the first time during Mass at a Roman Catholic church in a nearby village. After the Mass, I visited and received blessings from several neighbors who meant a great deal to me. My mother set up an altar in our small living room, and I sat in front of the altar, which was decorated with a linen cloth, two tall candles, and a rosary. I recited the rosary several times during the day and said short prayers. From an early age, I learned the discipline of going before God. At bedtime, I would continue this discipline by kneeling by my bed before God. I would often fall asleep before my prayer ended, in which case, my mother would gently steer me into my bed.

My mother cleaned, cooked, washed our clothes by hand, and did all the ironing. I vowed that, when I was older and able, I would help her with the household chores. On rainy days, I would wear my father's rain boots on the wet, muddy backyard as I did my daily chores of feeding the poultry: ducks, fowls, turkeys, and chickens. At night, we would pen up the poultry in many little, handmade houses grouped three to six together to protect them from animals waiting to make them their prey. Squirrels and birds also had their little hideouts in their cages. I would hold my breath so as not to inhale the stench coming from the houses as I opened them to change the beds and to give the animals feed and water.

Raising poultry was not unusual for families in my country. It was a joy to hear the "gobbling" noise of the turkeys and to see and hear the ducks flap their wings as they bathed in the pond we had made. I got the chance to see turkeys, fowls, and ducks give birth to their little ones. As the time drew near for their babies to be born, their eggs would become darker and, little by little, the babies would break through the eggs. Sometimes, I would help the birth process by breaking just a piece of an eggshell. Joy came when, for example, six yellow ducklings were born and were strong enough to walk to the pond in single file behind their mother in order to learn the skills of bathing, flying, and eating. For Christmas, we would choose the fattest turkey, duck, and fowl or a combination of any two kinds of poultry for our dinner. I would sadly help my mother butcher them in preparation for the holiday meal.

As a young girl, I loved the outdoors and enjoyed playing typical games for girls my age, like hopscotch and jump rope. However, I did not participate in a sport at school. In my teenage years, my parents allowed me to go on monthly picnics with friends at the Royal Botanic Gardens in Trinidad, which are located in Port-of-Spain just north of the Queen's Park Savannah. The landscaped site occupies 62.8 acres and contains some 700 trees.[6] I enjoyed the beauty of the flowers, the birds, and the hills. I often climbed hills and would experience leg cramps afterward, to the point that I would cry from the pain. When our church organized a beach trip, my mother allowed me to go, but only after issuing strict warnings:

"Be careful, yuh hear? Don't go too far out. The waves are strong, yuh know, and I don't want anything to happen to yuh, yuh hear?"

My mother was afraid that I might drown in the strong tidal waves. I believe she had a problem at the beach when she was little, and she never forgot it.

When I was old enough, I kept my vow and helped my mother around the house, cooking and cleaning, ironing clothes, and doing some house painting during the holiday season. I particularly enjoyed gardening: planting a seed, watching the seed grow into a plant, and seeing a whole crop evolve from one seed. We planted corn, tomatoes, spinach, dasheen, and other vegetables. We also had mango trees, and I loved to jump up and pick a mango.

As a teenager, I loved both learning and teaching others, so I tutored my cousin and our neighbor's two children in English and Mathematics for free. I particularly enjoyed the routine of attending school, going to the library after school, and taking examinations and wondering if I had passed them. When I became overwhelmed with studies my father decided to hire a helper to assist my mother with washing and ironing our clothes; so that I could be relieved of those duties. From that time forward, school became my manner of life and my passport to my independence and freedom. My parents encouraged me to further my studies and go abroad. I knew the day would come when I would graduate from home.

Prayer:

I thank You, Father, God of the Universe.[7]
Thank You for all Your many blessings.
Thank You for the beauty of the ocean,
Sunshine, stars, trees, flowers, and birds.
I thank You for the nurturing that
I received from my parents.
Thank You for helping me to be
Submissive to their authority.
Now, Lord,
I pray that You would open doors
So I can walk in my destiny.
In Jesus' name, Amen.

The Lord's reply:

"The Mighty One, God, the Lord,
speaks and summons the earth
from the rising of the sun to the
place where it sets.
From Zion, perfect in beauty,
God shines forth."[8]

"See, I have placed before you an
open door that no one can shut.
I know that you

have little strength,
yet you have kept my word, and have
not denied My name."[9]

Reflection:

I had learned obedience from an early age. Now, I was asking God to enlarge my territory. I was asking Him to get me out of the box and free me up.

Your reflection:

Do you remember a time in your life when you wanted freedom? Jot down why you wanted freedom. How did you use the freedom you obtained? How have you learned from your experiences?

2

Leaving Home

Going abroad was no small matter to me. It meant the possibility of going to college, landing a job, and making a way for my family members and myself. I could have relinquished the idea of going abroad, but what did I have to lose? Staying in Trinidad meant competing with the brightest students for a seat at either the University of Trinidad or Jamaica. Then, there was the difficulty of obtaining a job right out of the university. My father, advanced in years and the breadwinner, had a job that was uncertain. He was always struggling to make ends meet and was totally unable to afford the cost of a college education. My father was a shipping clerk who checked in daily at the Port-of-Spain wharf for work, and he, at times, sadly returned home without a day's work. On those disappointing days, my mother would comfort him with: "John, don't worry about it; God will see us through."

When I told friends, family, and neighbors that I was going abroad, they packed into our two-bedroom home to give me their farewell hugs and best wishes.

Ms. Thelma, our neighbor across the street, said, "Joan, yuh parents are dependin on yuh to do well; don't let dem down, now. When yuh in trouble, don't forget to call on duh name of God, yuh hear?"

I was tired of listening to people's advice and, worse yet, their expectations. My thoughts were, "Are these people setting me up for failure?"

However, I humbly took their advice and, with mixed feelings, pictured myself in a world with newly found freedom, leaving the old world illuminated by all of its beauty and yet darkened by our parents' inherent structure and control and the subsequent boredom under which we children lived.

I was leaving Trinidad and Tobago, the place of my birth, where I had grown up with the security and love of my parents, extended family, and neighbors, a community of people who loved and cared for me, appreciated me, and understood me, and was going to a place where I knew no one. I was twenty-three years old at the time but was still living at home. The thought of leaving everything and everyone behind was frightening, but I took the risk and pretended that I was going on an adventure. The feeling of adventure initiated excitement in me and readied me for what lay ahead.

My parents encouraged me, tailored warm pajamas and two-piece skirt-suits, assisted me with the money for my flight, and provided me with $500 US for traveling money. I did the needed research and decided that I wanted to go to Boston to live, work, and attend college. I learned of a residence located in the South End of Boston, and applied for a room there. They referred me to a YWCA, located on Clarendon Street where I stayed temporarily until the residence had a vacancy.

My flight to the United States was my first plane ride, so I was a bit nervous. I prayed at times and put my fingers in my ears to ward off the funny feeling I experienced when the plane was either ascending or descending. At night, sparkling lights from the skyscrapers produced picturesque and scenic views of New York and Boston.

"This is certainly different," I thought.

I arrived in Boston, safe and sound, on October 27, 1968, after a seven-hour flight that I was glad had ended. I got to the luggage pickup and suddenly realized that I had no one to receive me. I walked briskly but cautiously to the front gate and hailed a taxi to the local YWCA, where I was staying temporarily. Back on the island, I had heard strange stories of bad things happening to good people, and that thought frightened me somewhat. I thought the best way to handle the driver was to talk to him a lot. I proceeded to ask him, "Are you from here?"

He said, "No," and continued to drive, paying close attention to the steering wheel and the tunnel that we were approaching.

I continued, "Where are you from, then?"

"I am from Haiti," he said. "I studied in Haiti and came here to make it better for my family there."

"Wow, I came here to do the same," I responded. "This is my first time traveling, and I am looking forward to my stay here. The place I am staying is on Clarendon Street."

"At last, I'm in America!" I exclaimed. I was going to the United States to work and attend college. I had not yet applied for a job or college and had no idea how my plans would materialize. However, I was determined to persevere and attain my goals, regardless of how long it would take me to achieve them.

Before long, we got to my destination, and I was safe. I got out of the taxi, thanked the driver for a safe journey, paid him, giving him a $2 tip for his service, and proceeded to the front desk.

I approached the front desk, gave my name, paid the balance I owed, was handed my key, and was told to go to the seventh floor. The women at the desk were friendly. The first question one asked me was, "Do you sing?"

I said, "Oh no, I wish I did."

Her reply was, "You have a beautiful voice, and I like your accent too."

"Thank you."

"Do they speak English in Trinidad?"

"Yes, we do. People believe that we speak another language because of the different ethnic backgrounds present on our island. There are blacks, Indians, Chinese, Spanish, whites, mixed races, and other nationalities."

When I was finished speaking with the receptionist, I took the elevator to my room. The ride in the elevator seemed endless. There was no one in there but me. As I exited the elevator, I shuddered at the thought of walking down the dark, gloomy hallway, passing closed doors and not even hearing the sound of voices. I grappled with my loneliness. I opened the door and anxiously and eagerly walked into my room, not knowing what I would find there. The room was small, neat, and comfortable, with a twin bed, a small bureau, a telephone, a desk, and a chair, but with little room to walk around. I left the room with key in hand for a minute or two, hoping that by chance I would come across someone in the hallway, but, to my utter disappointment, there was no one—no Mammy, no Daddo to talk to, no neighbors to call out to. No one.

For the next two or three minutes, fear engulfed me. I decided to put the bolt on the door for protection, go under the covers, and cry myself to sleep. Thoughts flooded my mind. "I came to America to better myself, to further my education, to help my parents, my siblings, to make a way for all of us. There is no need to cry. This is your first day in America, give yourself time." Just then, I thought of a better way to deal with my fear. "What do I have to lose if I pray?" I thought—so I prayed to God. I don't remember saying too much. . .

Prayer:

Lord, if You are there,
Please make Yourself known to me.
I am here alone, and I am afraid.
I have taken a huge step by coming to America.
I don't have anyone to talk to except to You.
I need You, Lord, to help me through this process.
I just do not know where to begin.
Please help me!
I pray in Jesus' name, Amen.

The Lord's reply:

"For I am the Lord, your God, who takes
hold of your right hand and says to you,
'Do not fear; I will help you.' "[1]

My reply:

I thank You Lord,
For Your guidance.[2] strength,[3] and hope.[4]
Thank You for coming to
My rescue when I need You.
Thank You for Your
Love and care.[5]

Reflection:

Immediately, I felt the warmth and security of my God. I called my parents that night and discussed my flight and my room. With joy, I reassured them that I was in good hands. I was in good hands, because God was taking care of me.

Your reflection:

Reflect on how you have handled moments of fear and loneliness. Pray and commit your fear and loneliness to God.

3

Starting Over

After two weeks, I moved from the YWCA on Clarendon Street to the residence where I had pre-registered. The residence was a large community building with brightly lit single rooms conveniently located in the South End of Boston not far from an MBTA stop. The front foyer was beautifully carpeted and included an array of large green plants, which enhanced its beauty. The residence was an exciting place for me to live; I was able to live alone, enjoy my privacy, and yet, be in the company of others. It gave me an opportunity to learn new things and meet new people. I learned how to live in community from the friendships I gained, friendships, that I had no idea would last for a lifetime.

The women and I were single-working women; the residence afforded us comfort and a safe environment to live. We had breakfast and dinner, shared the laundry room, and had Sunday tea and brunch together. The Sunday tea was special; tea was served by 3 p.m. in special silverware. We were not allowed to wear slacks for tea or dinner. We had a curfew of 11 p.m. during the week and 12 p.m. on weekends. It was interesting to watch and admire other women as they went to the next level in their relationships, as their dates brought flowers for them and took them out to dinner. Eating was difficult on the weekend, when meals were not served at the residence. Many of the women chose to utilize a restaurant a few miles away, go downtown to eat, purchase light snacks from the tiny mom and pop stores nearby, or go on dinner dates on Sunday evenings, travel alone, or with a friend if one was left.

I used the $500 US that my father had given me carefully and wisely. I quickly learned the subway by trial and error and, before long, was applying for jobs. I applied to banks because they were more accessible by train, or within walking distance, and easier for me to secure an entry-level position.

Five weeks later, I obtained a clerical position at a local bank in Boston. I had been at the job no more than a month when I looked up and saw Carl taking a tour of the very bank where I was working. I recognized his six-foot figure, long gait, serious facial expression, and calm composure. We had been close friends in Trinidad, dated for a short time, and then I had left to come to America. I was very surprised to see him. I stared at him long and hard, then looked down and continued doing my work. I looked up again and realized he was coming my way. His eyes and mine met, and I knew at that moment that God had ordained our meeting. Carl came over to my desk, and I remember saying, "I didn't know that you were in Boston. When did you come, and how long are you staying?"

With a grin, he said, "I came in October. I usually visit, but I think this time, I will be staying for good." We exchanged numbers and addresses, and he kept in touch with me.

Carl was a typical gentleman. During our high school days, he and I would meet frequently at a taxi stand and talk as we both waited for a taxi. That is how we became friends. We would ride the taxi together, and Carl would pay for my ride. My parents were impressed by Carl's gentlemanliness. However, if you knew my parents, especially my father, you would know that it would take a running bull to change his ideas and feelings about his daughters' relationships with male friends. My father felt that our studies mattered more than talking and spending time with boyfriends. When our boyfriends did visit, my father would sometimes interrupt our conversations with them, to our embarrassment. He would say the craziest things like, "Hello, I don't want any panorama in here." He was continually suspicious of our intentions and concluded that it was unusual for two people to simply sit and talk.

But Carl was a strategist. He would make a point to visit me at my parents' home on major holidays, when love and joy abounded everywhere, when strangers and distant relatives were welcomed in our home. Carl never telephoned me before he came to visit, but somehow, I knew when to expect him.

When he visited me, my parents always welcomed him. My mother would always say, "Carl, yuh want some cake and some sweetbread?"

He would always reply, "Thanks, Ms. Moses." Carl was never shy when it came to black cake and sweetbread. Carl loved black cake and sweetbread both then and now.

I remember the questions that flooded my head when I was in Trinidad: Whom would I marry? Which young man would fit my profile? I was thinking of having a family some day if the Lord willed. I knew Carl and I would have joy in our lives, but we had no idea of the difficulties that lay ahead.

Prayer:

God Almighty, God of all Wisdom and Knowledge,[1]
The Author and Finisher of my Faith,[2]
The God Who knows best for me,[3]
I do not want to wait forever Lord, for the right one
Or rush into a relationship with the wrong person.
I come asking You Lord, to show me the right person.
I pray in Jesus' name, Amen.

The Lord's reply:

"Trust in the Lord, and do good;
dwell in the land, and enjoy safe
pasture.
Delight yourself in the LORD
and he will give you the desires of
your heart."[4]

Reflection:

God knows everything before we ask Him,[5] even who is best for us. If it is God's will for you to be married, in due time and season, He would orchestrate your life and send you His best. Wait on God. Deep in my heart, I knew that God was preparing me to be Carl's wife. I pictured life with him and our many children together in a large country home with lots of trees, livestock, and animals.

Your reflection:

Reflect on an area in your life where you explored new beginnings. Describe what you had to give up. What have you learned from making correct choices?

4

Attending College

My associate's degree from a two-year business school in Trinidad helped me secure admission to a major university in Boston and study only two and a half years to fulfill the requirements for a bachelor's degree. I was surrounded by positive people at the residence who encouraged me to pursue my dream of attending a four-year college. One of the women from the residence invited me to dinner at the home of one of her relatives and surprised me with a gift of $300 toward my college education. I was truly grateful.

When I was accepted to the university, I could not hold back the tears that rolled down my cheeks. They were tears of joy. How I was to attend this major college without money was the sixty-four thousand dollar question. I did not have the answer. However, after meeting with financial aid personnel and learning that I would receive school loans and a work-study package, I was much more at ease.

College was challenging, with reading and homework assignments, quizzes, mid-terms, and final examinations. In 600-person auditoriums,

I was lost if I did not take good notes, so if I missed any portion of a lecture, after class, I would compare notes with another student. I lived and worked on campus, working ten hours a week at the business office to assist me with my daily expenses. During holidays like Thanksgiving, students like myself who were not visiting their families, were transferred to a dormitory further away from the main campus. That posed additional problems for me, since there were no cafeteria services, no restaurants nearby, no friends with whom to link up, and no car with which to travel. I was hungry and lonely. On Thanksgiving Day, in 1969, I walked the streets near the confines of the dormitory in search of restaurants, but there were none—only variety stores serving small sandwiches, snacks, and soft drinks. In desperation, I bought a sandwich, a bag of chips, and a Pepsi and returned to my room. Memories of my first day in America surfaced. However, I made it through Thanksgiving Day, 1969.

I had no one to turn to except for God, Who continually reassured me that I was not alone, that He was with me, and that He would take care of all of my needs. All I had to do was depend on Him.

In the days, weeks, months, and years following, I was determined to study hard, maintain good grades, and graduate with my Bachelor of Science degree. I was always in the library catching up and studying for midterms and final examinations. On one occasion, while studying for a midterm, I was awake with fellow students till mid-morning. When I entered the classroom, I knew I could not sit for the examination. I had a throbbing headache and asked the professor for a makeup examination. I was under pressure, particularly during my first semester. The Dean of the university explained that my transfer was dependent on my grade average my first semester. Of course, I believed him, so I made the Dean's List that first semester. I never heard from him my first or second semester. I believe he wanted me to do well.

The workload in college continued to be overwhelming, but I knew I had to persevere or be a failure. I prayed to God concerning my examinations:

Prayer:

Lord God, Omnipotent Father,[1]
I magnify your great name.[2]
I confess my feeling of inadequacy.
I repent of this feeling, Lord.
Please forgive me for the way I feel.
Thank You for Your greatness in my life.[3]
Lord, I face the issue of failure in my life.
I am struggling in some
Areas and doing very well in others.
I pray Lord, that You would give me
Strength and wisdom to do well
In college.
In Jesus' name, Amen.

The Lord's reply:

"Not by might nor by power,
but by my Spirit."[4]

Reflection:

I trusted God in everything. If I got a "C" on a particular examination, I would make an appointment with the professor and review the examination to see how I could improve. By the end of the course, I had mastered areas where I was weak. God had given me perseverance and strength to overcome my difficulties. God was my helper in my time of need. All I had to do was ask, and I received.

Your reflection:

What difficulties are you experiencing at this time? Pray and release them to God. He will order your steps. He will give you the strength to overcome your difficulties. As you pray, write down step-by-step instructions you receive from God concerning your situation.

5

Celebrating Birthdays, Christenings, and Holidays

Tony, our first child, Rese, our second, and Monique, our third, were all born in the seventies followed by Jo-An who was born in the middle eighties. We were truly happy to have two sons and two daughters. Life was enjoyable.

My extended family, mother, father, and two sisters came to Boston in 1972, so Carl and I had a community to fall back on. When our children were born, our extended family members provided the needed daycare services for us. During the period of our children's births, my four sisters and brother were also having children, so christening and birthday parties happened everywhere. We celebrated christening and birthday parties to commemorate our children's births, God's gifts to us. At four to six weeks after each birth, we would have a christening ceremony for our new baby, which was celebrated in a local church before family, friends, and god-parents. The godparents would stand with us at the altar, and one of them would hold our child. The minister would recite prayers and charge the godparents and parents to bring up the child in the ways of the Lord. He would bless the child, and then the ceremony would end. It was typical for families to take pictures of the ceremony. After the ceremony, a celebration would follow at our home. Food and drink included pelau, macaroni pie, potato salad, roti, black cake (which resembled a wedding cake), and fruit punch.

Extended family and friends frequented our home for our children's birthday parties. Tony and Rese's birthdays were one week apart, so we held one party for both boys. Now I understand that was not a good idea, since Tony did not feel special as a result. Our sons' party was simpler than our daughters.' They would invite their friends, eat, talk, and laugh, and that was the end of it. There were never sleepovers, and that was a relief.

As our sons got older, we decided to install a basketball hoop outside to keep them busy—wrong move! The boys from the neighborhood lived at our home after that. My home office, situated at the rear of the house, was home to the noise of, "Yes! Yes!" or, "I told you I would win!" signifying affirmations of victory. I lived through every exclamation, glad at times to listen to the constant bursts of laughter and joy, and the trotting of the feet that was indicative of the game. As I sat there listening, I could not help but remember my life, smothered with so much structure that I did not have opportunities to have fun, so although the noise disturbed me until I had no peace, when I looked at their faces beaming with laughter and joy, I couldn't say, "I think it's time for you boys to end the game."

The party for our younger daughter, Jo-An, was simple. She had sleepovers every year except for one occasion, when her party was at Chuck E. Cheese. She would invite the same four girls yearly, her two cousins and two friends. For entertainment, she always had "pin the donkey" and musical chairs.

Our older daughter's party could be a sleepover, a cookout, or a pool party. Monique loved variety. Our home turned into a playground when there was a sleepover. The children played with water balloons on hardwood floors, and we adults would stand there, doing nothing until the hardwood floors got slippery and it was time for parental intervention: "Girls, I think it's time to stop the water balloons now. You might fall and hurt yourselves."

"Ok."

When it was time for the girls to go to bed, Carl and I would quietly retreat to bed, open-eyed, hoping to hear snoring. Instead, we would hear a never-ending rumble as the girls indulged in pillow fights and endless chattering and laughter. On one occasion, one child cried all night because she had forgotten to bring her security blanket.

"I want my security blanket; I want my security blanket!" she cried.

"Well, sweetheart, your mother forgot to bring it, but I can give you another blanket," I said.

"No, I want my security blanket!"

No blanket in the world could substitute for her security blanket, so I played the role of mother, hugging and consoling her.

When we held the party at Burger King, it was not as much fun as a sleepover but I did not have to clean up. Unfortunately, Monique hurt herself on the swings outside! We just couldn't win. Since Monique's birthday fell on Memorial Day, and as she grew older, she opted to have cookouts at our home. As parents, we felt no obligation to have birthday parties for our adult children, but we loved the idea of getting together with family and friends to share, laugh, and enjoy one another.

While the May cookouts continued to be lots of fun, I was always completely exhausted from the enormous amount of food preparation, cleaning, and rearranging that I did in preparation for them. The main course was always pelau (rice and peas with chicken), curry and barbeque chicken, and potato salad. I would do all of the shopping, but Carl did all of the last-minute shopping for items such as ice, candles, paper plates, cups, forks, knives, sodas, and other miscellaneous items. Carl would also do the barbequing, although he did not enjoy doing it. Our friends would arrive early to talk and share, while extended family and others would arrive much later. Our daughter would entertain her cousins as late as 10 p.m. I never knew when the party ended, for I would usually retreat to bed about 9 p.m.

Christmas, New Year's Eve, and Easter were festive times in our country, times to renew relationships, and, most of all, times to thank God for all that He had done and was still doing in our lives. Christmas was a time of joy and excitement as family members did the traditional: visit everyone, eat, drink, laugh, and be joyous. At Christmas, we would open our doors to receive people dressed in red singing Christmas carols. The night would be young, and the songs of Christmas would resonate in our hearts, leaving us with peace and joy. Songs included "Joy to the World," which spoke about the coming of the Lord, the Savior of the world, who came to this earth to identify with, and make a way for us. New Year's Day was meaningful, the beginning of a new year. God had kept us safe through the past year. Easter was a symbol of the Resurrection, a time to enjoy the hope that Christ had given us through His death and resurrection. So as we remembered our tradition, we would prepare our homes and invite our families and friends to celebrate with us and they would reciprocate by inviting us to their homes. We would prepare traditional West Indian meals and drinks as a reminder of the island from which we came and Whom we served, our Lord and Savior, Jesus Christ. We would celebrate that joy with each other, embracing each other and showing our love for one another.

As I remembered my extended family, my prayer was:

Prayer:

Holy, Holy, Holy, Lord God of Hosts,
Heaven and Earth are filled with Your Glory.
Hosanna in the highest![1]
Lord, I confess the faults of my family members
And all of my faults.
I repent of all of our sins.
Father, please forgive us for our errors.
I thank You for the victory You have afforded us
As a result of the Cross.[2]
Lord, I pray for my immediate and extended
Family members,
That You would draw them to You.
I do not pray for these only,
But also for friends, acquaintances,
And others throughout the world,
That You would draw them to Yourself,
That they would acknowledge You as their Lord

And Savior even in the midst of their difficulties.
In Jesus' name, Amen.

The Lord's reply:

"For God so loved the world that he gave his one and only Son, that whoever believes in him shall not perish but have eternal life."[3]

Reflections:

God hears and will answer our prayers in due time and season.[4] Although we feel that our prayers are in vain, we are planting seeds; others will water the seeds that we have planted. In due time, God will draw those, for whom we pray, to Himself.

Your reflection:

Reflect on your family and extended family relationships. If there are unresolved issues, ask God to take these burdens from you. Continue to pray for your family members.

6

Growing Up Years

When our children were much younger, I always maintained a flexible lifestyle: working full-time for awhile, teaching at a community college three days per week, and, at one time, operating a home-based consulting business. Carl was the breadwinner, working full-time and sometimes part-time to supplement the family's income. I did not bring in a whole lot of money, but my schedule allowed me to take our children to their medical and dental appointments and to spend quality time with them without feeling stressed. I loved to surprise them by dropping in during their classes to see how they were doing, to bring cupcakes to school on their birthdays, to drive them home from school on occasion, and to attend school plays, swim meets, and basketball games.

Tony, Rese, and Monique were getting older, entering middle school, changing and becoming more independent. Monique was involved in so many sports that she had difficulty keeping up with her homework. She was having the time of her life. Rese was doing well, particularly in French, English, and his extracurricular activities like music, basketball, and swimming. However, he had a temper with which to contend. Tony was doing well in the earlier grades but sometimes forgot to keep up with his homework. Carl and I were visiting our children's schools for teachers' conferences or speaking with teachers more frequently.

Those were challenging years for me. Carl gave the children and me the support that we needed: driving and accompanying me to parent and teachers' meetings and swim meets in the dark, dreary hours during winter season, and picking up our daughter Monique from cheerleading, basketball, or track practice.

Before we ever thought of having cookouts, my husband Carl and I drove up to Rese's school on Memorial Day and actually marched in the school band as Rese played the drums. Rese had an outgoing personality and could charm the dullest person. He excelled in everything he did. He played the guitar and drums, swam, and participated in basketball. In the 1980s, we had occasion to witness his First Communion at his local Roman Catholic school. Rese, now about six feet tall, was dressed in a white suit. Anyone could see his good-looking, dimpled face and convincing smile a mile away.

He was stubborn at times. I remember that when he was fifteen, Carl and I drove him to a swim meet, and he refused to swim.

"Go in the water Rese," I said. "You are not going to waste our time here."

After several promptings, he angrily jumped into the water but did not swim his best. He came out saying, "I told you; I didn't want to swim, but you guys kept forcing me to do it!"

When Rese was sixteen, he begged me once to let him drive my car.

"Mammy, I am not going far; you can trust me."

I replied, "No, you are not driving my car, and that's that!"

My response did not stop him. Rese waited until I was asleep to use my car. The next morning, I awoke to find that my car had been in an accident and needed repairs. I was in tears knowing that I had purchased that used car not long ago and had to decide to either junk it or spend a lot of money repairing it. I chose to repair the car, which unfortunately, cost the same as the purchase price of the car.

We also visited Monique's school on several occasions to listen to her play the trumpet or to watch her participate in a play. Monique was the third child but the first girl, so she had to fend for herself and try to be as unique as possible. At one point, she was a tomboy playing GI Joe with her brothers. When she realized that she was still not considered part of their team, she networked with friends, participating in swimming competitions, track, and basketball tournaments. She would often stay over at friends' homes, since her high school was far away.

Monique was not as tall as her sister and her brothers. She had a medium height but a petite body that was strong. Very beautiful and photogenic, Monique enjoyed herself wherever she went. She was always the joy of any party; her face always looked radiant because of her beautiful smile. She knew how to laugh and bring joy wherever she was. I remember one shopping day when Monique was just about six years old that we could not find her in the Macy's Department Store basement (then Jordan Marsh Department Store). I was shopping for our sons' clothing, and Monique found an opportunity to hide under racks of clothes. She informed me later that she made believe the clothes were a forest filled with trees and that they had engulfed her. She came out of hiding to look for us, started crying, and, when she could not find us, went back to her hiding place.

Tony, our oldest son, was quiet and shy but was not quiet when it came to playing the piano. We loved to hear him play *The Entertainer* at his piano recitals. He was dark and tall, with a slim build and handsome features. He was also quiet, and reserved, sociable, and well-mannered, and he swam very fast and did extremely well at swim meets. He was the most obedient and respectful child of them all. He never talked back or disobeyed. I remember that when we would speak to him sternly about some issue, he would remain quiet and composed and look intently at us with his bright brown eyes. All three children were great at swimming, so they kept us quite busy with meets at different places and at different times.

Everyone remembers me pushing Jo-An in her stroller. Jo-An attended a family daycare followed by a group daycare, which allowed me to maintain my teaching job three days per week. Jo-An was a very easy baby to care for. She drank her milk and juices and ate her cereals and food very well. I was sad that I could not continue to nurse her because of the surgery I had when she was three months old. I believe she missed the close nurturing that our other children received. A family video which was taken when Jo-An was about four years old showed that she did not seem to connect with other family members as the other children did, but was holding onto my skirt instead.

As Jo-An grew into a child of three, four, five years old, with large, black eyes, olive skin, and a peaceful demeanor, she was still the shy, sweet little girl who did not make a fuss about anything but just looked on. She continued to be with me at all times and under all circumstances. She enjoyed dancing classes at a local dancing school when she was five or six years old. She just had the figure for dancing, I thought, with that tall, slim figure, long legs, and pointed toes. She loved getting her face made up too, with lipstick and eye shadow, getting her nails done, and getting her hair pulled back into a bun.

As beautiful as our children were, we were constantly working hard to get them to understand the need to take responsibility for cleaning their rooms, helping in the kitchen and in the yard, and coming home on time.

We always heard from Monique: "Mammy, we are the only ones who do not go downtown alone or go to a friend's house after school."

We were adamant about her coming straight home after school. "I do not care what other people do. We want to know where you are at all times, and your place is at home. You have homework and chores to be done as well."

She often stayed in her room and slept while leaving the television on. Oh, how angry that behavior made me feel; the electric bill was increasing. "Does this girl understand what it means to turn off the lights?" I would think to myself.

Rese was a constant challenge. He did not want anyone to talk to him. Often when I came home from work, he would be leaving so he wouldn't have to hear what I had to say.

"Rese, did you clean your room!? I am not going to stand for any nonsense."

"Yes, Mammy."

Tony was very quiet, and I had to remind him constantly: "Tony, did you do your weekly chores?"

He would quietly respond, "I know, I know, Mammy, I'll do them later."

As Tony, Rese, and Monique grew in stature and were about to go to college, it began to get more difficult to pin them down to any task. They were simply normal teenagers with their own agendas.

My prayer:

O Lord my God, my help in the time of need,[1]
I confess that I feel overwhelmed and
Guilty for being a strict parent.
I repent of my sins.
Please forgive me, Lord, for my sins.
I thank You for giving me strength[2]
And the ability to discipline our
Children.
I pray for direction and wisdom
As we interact with our children daily.
In Jesus' name, Amen.

The Lord's reply:

"Train a child in the way he should go,
and when he is old, he will not turn from it."[3]

Reflection:

I reflect on our past disciplinary actions. I am glad that Carl and I stood our ground. Now, our adult sons and daughters turn to us for counsel.

They are grateful for how they were raised and nurtured.

Your reflection:

Reflect on issues you face or have faced while caring for a loved one, raising your children, nieces, nephews, younger siblings, or cousins, or while teaching school children. What steps are you taking or have taken to resolve your issues? Write your reflections here.

7

Visiting Nova Scotia-1986

My friend from the residence was kind enough to make her family cottage available to us, so in August, 1986, our entire family traveled to Nova Scotia, Canada. Jo-An was almost 3 years old then, Monique 9, Rese 12, and Tony 14. Jo-An was walking, running, talking, so it was easier for us all.

Our station wagon, which we called our "green machine," was old and rusty. When we started packing our luggage and putting the bicycles on the bicycle rack, I was certain that our car would not make it to Maine. I was nervous the whole time, particularly because we had only enough time to drive there and catch the boat. Carl drove our old station wagon to Portland, Maine, and at approximately 9 p.m., we boarded the *Scotia Prince* with our four children. I knew that going on a trip of that nature, with the entire family, was a handful, but since I had never gone on a boat ride for such a long distance, I thought it would be exciting. I could not wait to go. The cabins on the boat were adequate, with double beds and room enough for our family. This was new. Different.

Although I experienced seasickness, the journey to Nova Scotia for me was not bad, because I slept through most of the night. On our return journey to Maine, I also felt sick from the constant movement of the boat. On our way to Nova Scotia, the food was so good; however, that I attempted to eat a salad, not knowing it was a lobster salad. For a moment after eating the salad, I thought I would faint because of my allergic reaction to shellfish, but luckily, I managed to stay strong. The children enjoyed the many games on the boat.

While Carl was driving through Nova Scotia in search of my friend's family cottage, our daughter Monique needed to use the bathroom. We knocked at someone's door. A woman came to the door, and we politely asked, "Ma'am, can we please use your bathroom? Our daughter needs to go badly."

Surprisingly, the owner opened her door, invited us in, and said, "Certainly, come right in. I'll show you to the bathroom."

"Thank you so much. You are so kind," I said.

"You seem to have come a long way."

"Yes, we traveled from Boston, took the *Scotia Prince* from Portland, Maine, and have a distance to go yet before we come to our friend's family cottage." She told us the unique spots to visit and wished us well on our vacation.

We arrived at my friend's family cottage. My family and I remembered the cottage after twenty-two years, as one which sat on a hill overlooking a pond and the ocean. It was a three-bedroom suite with bunk beds and a master bedroom, full bath, kitchen, living room, and dining room. The appliances were practically new, the furniture wooden, sturdy, and in very good condition. The house included a veranda furnished with white garden chairs and overlooking a garden filled with beautiful flowers that brought a feeling of relaxation, and that compensated for the darkness that we experienced inside because of the all-wood furniture. Sitting on the veranda, with rays of sunshine coming through the windows, the beauty of the brightly colored flowers, and the friendliness of the people, I pictured myself in Trinidad.

A wooded path from the backyard led to the pond and, a few yards beyond, was the ocean where the family went daily; we walked into the water up to our waists; the water was warm from the constant sun and clear from the blue skies arching over it, so clear that we could see our reflections in it. At times, Jo-An and I would stay at the pond area or I would be involved in teaching her to ride her tricycle.

When we arrived in Nova Scotia, our boys, Tony and Rese, quickly took their bikes off the bicycle rack and toured the neighborhood! Our daughter Monique and my husband Carl quickly located the ocean and had a quick swim. They complained often of being bitten in the water and could not understand what was biting them, because the water was so clear! Monique found a friend, and together, they would search for frogs and grasshoppers, which Monique considered packaging to take home.

Monique kept coming to me and shouting, "Mammy, my friend and I searched and found frogs. The frogs are different in these parts. They look smaller! I found a grasshopper! Look, I am going to put it in a jar and take it home. Do you think it will live until we get home?"

"I don't think so, Monique. I think the grasshopper needs air just like we do."

Jo-An was fascinated with butterflies.

"Mammy, look—a butterfly."

"Jo-An, we have lots of butterflies in Trinidad. Do you remember seeing them? You were probably too young to remember."

Just then, our sons came rushing in: "Mammy, we had so much fun! This place is so quiet and peaceful. It reminds me of Trinidad. I like the people too."

"Where did you guys go?"

"We rode all around the neighborhood. We got too far and decided to return before we got lost. It was fun!"

Carl and I reviewed the situation. It would cost a lot to take our children out to eat three times per day, so Carl opted to buy groceries, and unfortunately, I agreed to cook at the cottage.

"Ok, Carl, as much as I feel like having a vacation, I give up—I will cook simple meals. Will you help me clean?"

"Whatever."

"That's not an answer."

"I will. I will. Just enjoy yourself and stop worrying."

While we were there, we visited a lighthouse and some small shops. We took walks. We prepared meals at the cottage. Carl, the children, and I had a good time. As I reflect now, I don't remember ever having had a better time. Our entire family was together, and everything was beautiful.

Prayer:

This is the day the Lord has made;
We will rejoice and be glad in it.[1]
Lord, I confess my lack of faith

Visiting Nova Scotia-1986

When I did not think we would make it to Maine.
I repent of my lack of faith.
Lord, please forgive me for my sin.
Father, thank You for protecting us[2] as we traveled to Maine.
You kept the car from breaking down.
Thank You for Your loving care and Your tender mercy.[3]
You allowed the woman to open her door for us when we needed help.
Thank You for providing a place for our entire family to stay,
And for creating the scenery that would give us peace and quiet
And would usher us into Your presence.[4]
I pray that You would be glorified in the coming days.
In Jesus' name, Amen.

The Lord's reply:

"For the Lord God is a sun and shield;
the Lord bestows favor and honor;
no good thing does he withhold
from those whose walk is blameless."[5]

Reflection:

Regardless of how old the station wagon was, we made the trip and caught the boat on time. It was God Who made it possible for us to have a successful trip.

Your reflection:

Have you taken a recent trip, took one in the past, or intend to take one? Take a moment and jot down what you liked most about your trip or what you want from a trip you are currently planning? What have you learned from a trip you have taken? How can you incorporate those happy moments into your daily life?

8

Taking Day Trips

Day trips included shopping trips, medical appointments, church, and mini-outings. Since my husband Carl worked full-time and part-time on the weekends, when it was time to purchase school clothes, I would go to the store with all four children. On those shopping days, each child was allotted $150.00, and each picked out his or her clothes, except for Jo-An, who was much younger.

Shopping days were fun but a bit overwhelming—I could have used another hand. While our sons picked out their clothes, I would help the girls. After shopping, we always sat down to a meal. When it was time to fetch the car from the parking lot, I just couldn't ever remember where I had parked, so I would walk up and down the parking lot trying to find my car.

I would arrange medical appointments for our sons on one day and for our daughters on another. We always had a meal in the hospital cafeteria before heading home.

Church was much easier. We attended a Baptist church conveniently located one block from our home. This church was large, with brightly colored stained glass windows so the sun could be seen when we were having service. The church had the most unique set up for baptism right there behind the pulpit. There was a stained glass window with a picture of Jesus beckoning one to come and be baptized. I remember always walking in with a bag of eatables and activities for the younger ones to do. It worked every time. I always had enough to give to another child whose mother was having a hard time. Our children loved the church, since they were involved in children's church and Sunday school classes, had occasions to sing before the church, interacted with their childhood friends, and particularly enjoyed the food that was served in the fellowship hall following the service.

Mini-outings included visits to local zoos and parks, the library, and annual day trips to Martha's Vineyard. On the weekends when Carl did not work, he would often take us to local and out-of-state parks and beaches such as Nantasket Beach, Houghton's Pond, Canobie Lake, and others. He accompanied me to our children's swim meets, amusement parks, school plays, basketball tournaments, and musicals. He was very good with the children, helping to organize them for their swim tournaments, helping with picnics at parks or at beaches, swimming with the children, or taking the children riding up and down hills. Riding up and down hills was difficult for me; I just couldn't do that!

I looked forward to our annual day trip to Martha's Vineyard. I would drive to Woods Hole, park our car, and take a ferryboat over to the island. Our sons would take their bikes so they could ride and keep busy. Our daughter Monique would walk with me while I would push Jo-An in her stroller and view small shops. We would be mindful of the time but always stayed for the entire day, returning to Woods Hole by the last ferry-boat. We always had a splendid day!

I used every opportunity to take our children out so that I could have some fun at the same time. The Fourth of July was our biggest hit. Carl did not like classical music, but I did, so I thought: "Who can I think of to accompany me to hear the Boston Pops?"

That was easy. "Just take our children," I thought, and so I did. I took all four children and loaded their bikes onto our car. I got there early in the afternoon and foolishly parked my car in a no-parking zone.

The children rode over the BU Bridge while I pushed Jo-An in her stroller. They were excited! Since it was early, the children rode their bikes to and fro in the open space in front of the Hatch Shell, but as people began to assemble and sit on the grass, there was little space left for them to ride their bikes or spread their blankets. We spent a long time in the park, and by late afternoon had consumed all the food we had. Fortunately for us, there were people sitting next to us barbequing, and they shared what little they had with us. There were issues when it was time for the children to go to the bathroom, but we took care of that the best way we could. Later, after listening to and enjoying the Boston Pops and viewing the fireworks, we were ready to head home.

We walked on the bridge amid droves of people, the boys riding their bikes ahead of us. Monique was walking with her bike beside me while I pushed Jo-An in her stroller. It was late, and our goal was to get to our parked car as quickly as possible. We gave a sigh of relief as we approached the location of our car, our sons getting there before us. But where was our car? I was sure that I had parked it there! I had even memorized some landmarks.

"Mammy, I think our car was towed!" Rese blurted out.

"Let's call the police station," Tony suggested.

What were we to do? We turned around and walked toward a phone booth two or three blocks away and called the nearest police station. My boys, Tony and Rese, were still riding up and down the street while our daughter, Monique, was sitting on the ground holding her bike.

"Your car was towed, Ma'am, and you need to pay a $40 fine," I was told.

I called Carl immediately, and he made arrangements to pay the fine, pick up the car, and meet us at the 7/11 store. While waiting for Carl outside the store, we came into contact with a woman five feet six inches tall, olive in complexion, wearing her hair in a low afro style, and neatly dressed. Her eight-year-old son was walking beside her. She was swaying from side to side as she spoke to me, and her piercing eyes showed signs of desperation. She was frantic, eager to have her problems solved. She was pleading with me to take her child.

"Mem, could you take meh child?" As she said this, she pushed the child hurriedly to where our children were standing. The child was sobbing uncontrollably. For a moment, I remained stunned and speechless. Then to my utter amazement, she left her son where we were standing on the pavement and proceeded to walk away.

I said, "Ma'am, I can't take your child. I have to handle my own children. You can't leave your child here."

She continued to walk away busily, while her son, crying loudly and feeling lost and rejected, ran behind his mother and eventually caught up to her. I remember this woman and her child and wish that I could have offered her more assistance.

At that moment, our daughter, Monique, began to cry and said, "Mammy, let us go home. I'm scared. This woman seems crazy!"

Our sons exclaimed, "Mammy, let us get out of here right now!"

What could I do at that moment? I could not talk with this lady, although I wanted to. My children were frightened and upset. I had Jo-An in my arms. I had a full load. We needed to get home. When we did, the load was lifted. The children and I were safe. All I remembered was that I had a superb time with our children! The inconvenience did not matter.

Prayer:

Praises unto You, Mighty God, who sits on the throne.[1]
Father, God, I confess that I acted irresponsibly
When I parked our car illegally—wanting to enjoy myself, and
Not thinking of the consequences of my action.
I repent of this and ask you Lord, to
Please forgive me for my behavior.
Thank You for bringing us home safely.[2]
I pray that You would teach me, Lord,
To take one step at a time and to act wisely.
In Jesus' name, Amen.

The Lord's reply:

"If the Lord delights in a man's way, He makes his steps firm."[3]

Reflection:

I took a big step by taking four children to the Hatch Shell to listen to the Boston Pops play. I could have stayed for only a short portion of the day. When the food ran out, it was a signal for me to leave. Parking in an illegal parking spot was not a good idea, also. The scene with the mother trying to leave her son with me, and my trying to respond to that situation was impossible. I had four children of my own, and our car had been towed.

Your reflection:

Reflect on a time when you and your family had fun together, but messed up. What did you learn from your experience?

9

Graduating

The year 1994 marked a turning point in our lives. Monique graduated from high school that year, applied, and was accepted to a local college. I remember her graduation day; it was bright and sunny. Her graduation ceremony took place outside in the open field. Monique's supporters were her immediate family and lots of cousins. Her face lit up with radiant smiles as our group cheered, "Go Monique, Go Monique." After the ceremony, her face was wet with kisses, and her arms were filled with flowers. Everyone wanted a picture with Monique and got his or her wish. She was happy to see her immediate and extended family. She looked radiant and happy! We were proud of her as she moved to another level in her life.

Four years later, in May, 1998, she was graduating from college with her Bachelor of Science degree commemorating a great event in her life, as well as in ours. We looked forward to some joy in our lives, the joy of seeing a son or a daughter receive a degree from a college. Her ceremony was held inside. As Monique's name was about to be called,

I avoided the eyes of other spectators and moved closer so I could get to where she was getting her diploma, and yes, I got a good snapshot of her. We weren't as wild as we were for her high school graduation, but we were wild. "Hey, Hey, Hey," we exclaimed as she stood up. I had taken time to choose a beautiful bouquet of flowers for her. The bouquet included roses and lilies of bright Caribbean colors: yellow, orange, and pink. She had worked hard to graduate from high school and now college. We were proud parents. What great accomplishments for Monique! What joy! What freedom! Monique's graduation was so much fun. My youngest sister and her husband, nieces and nephews, and one of my friends attended the graduation. My husband Carl took our daughter, Jo-An, and came to the graduation later so I could get Monique to her graduation on time. They got lost in the crowd and were unable to find us.

Having Monique home again was fun, although she did not feel quite the same, since she had been used to her independence in college. She was returning home after having been away for four years and was plagued by rules and regulations again. We co-signed for her first car, agreeing to pay the monthly insurance premiums. She worked and made her car payments. Before long, she was attending graduate school. We supported her in that endeavor, because we were interested in her future. She finished her master of education degree and graduated in 2000.

Our oldest son, Tony, was serving as a reservist in the military once per month during the late nineties. He graduated from high school, applied, and was accepted to a local college. Tony and his fellow classmates were so happy on their graduation day from high school that they threw off their hats after they had received their diplomas. My mother, Agnes, whom I had sponsored in 1970, and who came to live in Boston in 1972,

Carl, Jo-An, and I later took our son to lunch. My mother had a wonderful time. She was not used to going out to eat, so she was elated.

Carl and I also attended Tony's college graduation. There was a sense of joy and excitement as the students took off their hats and threw them forward. We were excited for Tony as we screamed, "Go Tony, Go Tony." Tony was smiling and very happy. We took him out to eat afterward, and two of his cousins joined us. Tony was overjoyed that he had done extremely well. We were too. He had accomplished his dream of graduating from college. As with all our adult children, we helped Tony after graduation until he was able to be on his own.

Jo-An graduated from daycare and kindergarten in her earlier years but did not have a formal high school graduation. However, we celebrated many occasions with Jo-An, including her dance recitals, where she received flowers.

Rese, like Jo-An, did not have a formal graduation ceremony from high school, but we celebrated his many musical shows, where he played the guitar, the clarinet, and the drums.

Since my husband Carl completed his course work for his Bachelor of Science and Master's degrees later in the year, he felt that it was unnecessary to attend each graduation ceremony the following year.

I had the opportunity of graduating six months after my wedding with an undergraduate degree in business. I did not attend the ceremony the following year. Six years later, pregnant with our daughter Monique, I began taking courses that led to my Masters in Business Management degree. In 1981, I celebrated my graduation with my MBA degree, with my husband and my sisters at a seafood restaurant in Boston.

In 2004, I graduated from seminary with a Master of Arts degree, with a concentration in women's ministry. That was the best and greatest time of my life. In April of that year, I was surprisingly asked to attend an awards ceremony held at the seminary's main campus in South Hamilton, Mass., where I received The Robert J. Lamont Award for Academic Excellence. In the opinion of the faculty, the individual receiving the award was likely to apply his or her beliefs effectively to personal and social problems in the work of the pastorate.

On April 30, 2004, Carl and I attended a banquet at the Sheraton Ferncroft in Danvers, Massachusetts, and on May 1, 2004, my immediate family and friends surprised me by attending a banquet hosted by the local seminary where I attended. They bombarded me with flowers!

On May 6, 2004, the day before my graduation, I cleaned the house thoroughly, since our daughter Monique was staying at our home with Jo-An, and was taking her to the graduation luncheon. I had forgotten to buy a memory card for my digital camera. I thought I would do so when I arrived at South Hamilton later that night for the graduation church service. However, we got lost on the way and barely made it on time. I did not know how to erase some pictures and make room for others. I did not plan well. However, I had purchased a small camera for my husband to use to take pictures. He took pictures from far away!

The service was remarkable! We heard from two students who gave teary-eyed testimonies. The praise and worship time was awesome! We arrived at the hotel at approximately 10:30 p.m. I was exhausted and anxious, so I could not sleep. When I was about to fall asleep, my husband was waking up at his usual time of 4:30 a.m. to make his morning tea. I sobbed at the thought that I would not feel rested for my important day.

That morning, we started out on our trip once more. This time, we got there without any difficulty, because the day was sunny and bright. I got there in time for the group photo. Following the taking of the photo, we were asked to go to a certain building to receive a briefing on the graduation procedures. Carl met me as I was marching in with my fellow students and handed me my makeup bag, which did not contain my cell phone, my glasses or my camera, which we had accidentally left in the car.

My eyes hurt during the graduation ceremony. After the ceremony, all the graduates marched to another building to obtain their diplomas. All my friends, including Kate, then my daughter-in-law-to-be, took pictures as I left the ceremony. I truly felt loved and appreciated. In the midst of the excitement, I did not think to tell them, and neither did I have a cell phone to let them know, to which building I was headed to collect my diploma, so no one knew where Carl and I were. Carl faithfully remained at the building where the graduation ceremony was held, so he was able to find me when I returned to the building looking for everyone. Luckily, everyone remembered where we were going to have lunch, and we met up there.

When Carl and I got to the restaurant, we walked into the wrong room, where another party was celebrating, and everyone yelled out, "Congratulations! What college did you graduate from?" I told them of the seminary and the location, smiled, and quickly left the room, embarrassed. When we finally got to our room, overlooking the water, our entire party was there, waiting patiently: two of my friends and their husbands, and my immediate family.

Everyone presented me with gifts, which they insisted I open before lunch was served. Our table was filled with gifts and flowers, flowers of different colors: white and red roses, pink, orange, yellow, that added such beauty, such elegance and warmth to the occasion, a sign of everyone's love, care, and willingness to share my important moment with me. Our scrod dinner was cooked to perfection. We took pictures inside and outside, capturing the picturesque view of the restaurant overlooking the waters. My day was well spent.

Prayer:

Let everything that hath breath praise the Lord![1]
Lord, I confess that I haven't always been good
And deserving of Your blessings.
I repent Lord, and ask Your forgiveness for my
Thoughts and actions.
Thank You for the excitement of graduation.
We would not have made it
Without trusting and depending on You.
Thank You for family and supportive friends.
I pray that you would teach us to use the knowledge
That we have gained,
To the building up of Your kingdom.
In Jesus' name, Amen.

The Lord's reply:

"Give thanks to the Lord, call on his name;

make known among the nations what he has done.
Sing to him, sing praise to him;
tell of all his wonderful acts.
Glory in His holy name;
let the hearts of those who seek the Lord
rejoice."[2]

Reflection:

I look back and am at awe at how we all made it, in the midst of the challenges we faced at the time. I realize that the hands of God were holding us up.

Your reflection:

Reflect on the joyous moment of your graduation or that of a family member or friend. Describe your thoughts and feelings.

10

Getting Married, Celebrating Our Anniversary, and Carl's Birthday

Six months before my college graduation on February 20, 1971, Carl and I were married at a small Roman Catholic church in Boston before a small gathering of friends and relatives. I wore a white, satin gown with a pearl necklace and matching earrings. Carl rented a black tuxedo and wore a black bow tie. Our two bridesmaids wore bottle green velvet dresses. I was lucky to find a beautiful gown at a reasonable price, because neither of us could afford anything luxurious. Neither Carl's nor my parents were able to attend our wedding, but we had support from a great mix of friends and family. For our honeymoon, we spent two nights at a local hotel, since I was attending college and we could not afford an elaborate vacation.

Twenty-five years later, we were celebrating our wedding anniversary among family and close friends. Fifty people were in attendance, including our children, Tony, Monique, and Jo-an; my youngest sister, her husband, and their children; Carl's brother, sister, and niece. Everyone was happy, rejoicing, and really celebrating with us. Our church co-pastors officiated at the service, where we renewed our vows and rededicated our lives. Our reception was held in the basement of our church. As we walked down the aisle, my very good friend waved a scarf at me, signifying, "Go, Girl." In the basement, friends decorated the poles, giving them the appearance of large palm trees in the middle of an island. The walls were covered with pictures of Carl and me on our wedding day.

We remembered our younger daughter, Jo-An, on that anniversary day. She wore a floral dress with rose petals against a black background. Her hairstyle, which was dropped curls, were beaming in the light, and could be seen from a distance. Although Jo-An was shy, she managed to stand up and make a toast in front of family and friends. Monique wore a black, sleeveless dress and wore her hair in an up-do. With a radiant smile, she got up and said a few words to the audience. Our son Tony wore a black suit and white shirt and acted gentlemanly as he shook hands with relatives and friends. I was really proud of our children. Rese did not make it for our twenty-fifth anniversary celebration.

My husband Carl wore a beige suit, a beige tie, and a white shirt. I wore an off-white, knee-length wool suit, with a matching jacket that was beaded to the front, fitted, with a length just about two inches past my waistline. I found a pair of earrings resembling the pearls on my jacket. Our daughters and I each wore a bouquet of white roses, while my husband and son each wore a white rose boutonnière.

My youngest sister prepared various dishes for the event: curry chicken, barbeque chicken, rice and peas, Spanish rice, and barbeque ribs. People came up for seconds and thirds. People stood up and made comments concerning both Carl and myself, funny at times and, at other times, a bit embarrassing, but we got through them. We even had a photographer, who took pictures during the entire event. It was a day to remember!

We often celebrated our wedding anniversary with two nights in a local hotel. We would make the most of this wonderful time together. We would have fun participating in the hotel's buffet breakfast and going to dinner.

On October 5, 2002, I decided to give Carl a surprise birthday party. We went to our usual local hotel, so he did not suspect anything. I purchased a burgundy shirt for him, and I wore a blouse of the same color. As I was ironing Carl's jacket, I noticed that one button was missing. I realized that he had picked out the wrong jacket from the closet and that the vest that I had picked out was missing. We could not return home, because family members were at our house, preparing for the party. Luckily, the jacket was similar in color to the pants. The iron also left two spots on my shiny burgundy blouse. Carl kept telling me, "You worry too much. No one will see the spot. It's at night, and you will be sitting down to eat." I called every store in town to get another blouse, but every store was out of my size. However, after I put on the blouse, the spots were not obvious. Carl's new shoes were uncomfortable, so we returned them and secured another pair.

I told Carl that I had arranged to have dinner at a local hotel. When I got to the hotel where we were celebrating his birthday, I called my daughter Monique. "How is Jo-An?" I asked. This question was not a strange one, since Monique was caring for Jo-An so we could spend our anniversary together. I later stated, "Don't forget to cover her head." Usually this would mean to cover her head at night so her hairdo would stay in place. The two questions were codes that we had planned ahead of time, and they meant, "Carl and I are approaching the Madison room of the Sheraton Hotel; cover the sign on the outside door." When we entered the hotel room, everyone greeted Carl with a shout, "Surprise!!"

Carl was totally surprised! He gave Jo-An his jacket, because she was cold. Being without a jacket the entire night was not an issue for Carl. The music was a combination of oldies, some newer songs, and some songs for the young people in our midst. We danced and danced; we really enjoyed the night. We were not the only ones enjoying ourselves, for when I turned, I saw the smiles as everyone danced to the oldies with their husbands.

We returned to the hotel that night. I was glad that everything had worked out well. Carl was still surprised. Next morning, we had a wonderful breakfast with immediate and extended family members, some of whom had come from out of town for the event.

Prayer:

Jesus, Wonderful Counselor,[1]
I confess the sin of worry
And my need to please others.
I repent of these sins, Lord,
And pray that You would forgive me
Of my sins.
Thanks for working everything
Out according to your perfect will.[2]
Lord, teach me to relax and not
Be anxious about petty things.
Teach me to understand what

You are doing in our midst.
Help me to recognize You as
My Lord, my Savior, and my Hope.[3]
Show me how to enjoy life to the
Fullest without worry.
I pray these prayers in Jesus' name,
Amen.

The Lord's reply:

"Therefore, I tell you, Do not worry about your life, what you will eat; or about your body, what you will wear. Life is more than food, and the body more than clothes.[4]

For the pagan world runs after all such things, and your Father knows that you need them. But seek his kingdom, and these things will be given to you as well."[5]

Reflection:

Pleasing others at the expense of myself was always an issue for me. I spent a lot of time on the phone trying to get another blouse when I could have spent more time with my husband. Little things that I was upset about did not matter. What mattered most was us loving each other, and enjoying God's presence.

Your reflection:

Reflect on an important occasion in your life, when there was a lot of excitement and fussing. What was God teaching you through that experience?

11

Celebrating Our Son's Special Day

Our son Tony emerged from a quiet young person to a man with purpose. He knew what he wanted and took small, yet steady, steps to achieve his goals. Before starting college, he joined the military in 1994 as a reservist. The experience was tough, but, through it, he learned discipline, structure, and focus. By the time he graduated from college, he had satisfied the requirements of the military and was on his way to achieve other goals. He purchased his first home, and waited for the day when he would marry the right person. That day finally came on June 25, 2005, when he married Kate.

Family members on both sides were excited for the couple as we looked forward to their wedding day. The bride's family allotted us seventy-five seats, for which we were thankful. It was difficult deciding who to invite because of the size of our extended family and because everyone wanted to be there, but because it was impossible to please everyone, we concentrated on aunts and husbands and two adult children per household. My friends, dear to us, had witnessed Tony's growth from a small child to an adult and had to be counted. I felt a sense of excitement and fulfillment about the steps that our son had taken.

The bride and her parents planned the wedding, while my husband Carl and I paid for the rehearsal dinner and transportation. The actual rehearsal was fun and relaxing. We practiced walking down the aisle and joked when we made errors. Following the rehearsal, we had a scrumptious dinner of chicken, fish, and dessert. We viewed an entertaining video of Tony and his wife when they were growing up; it brought back memories when we saw my mother holding Tony as an infant.

Carl and I stayed overnight in a hotel with other wedding guests, including our daughter Monique, who was one of the bridesmaids. Jo-An was unable to attend the wedding because she was ill; a friend stayed at our home to care for her. Feeling nervous on the day of the wedding, I decided to wake up early to put on my makeup and secure help from Monique, if necessary. The limousine driver did his rounds in a timely manner, picking up the bridesmaids, then the ushers, Carl and myself, dropping off the bridesmaids and myself at the mother of the bride, Ann's, house, taking the ushers and Carl to the church, and finally taking the bridesmaids and myself to the church.

It was exactly 1 p.m. when we arrived at the church. It was 91 degrees, hot indeed, and the skies were blue. Family and friends were seated in a quaint country church with stained glass windows, Kate's family's church. No one seemed to bother about the heat as it threatened to smear the made-up faces of family and friends looking on and anxiously waiting for the bride.

The mothers walked in first. Carl accompanied me and her nephew Larry, accompanied Ann while the song, "You Raise Me Up," by Loveland

Graham was sung. Carl was dressed in a black tuxedo, grey vest, and white shirt, while I was dressed in a long, sky blue satin skirt with a slight tail, and a matching tailored jacket with gold sequins, Chinese color, and half-length sleeves. Ann wore a two-piece, pale pink dress and matching jacket. Larry, like the ushers, wore a black tuxedo, grey vest, and white shirt. As the song, "You and I," by Stevie Wonder was played, the best man, Rese, and the maid of honor, Paula, followed by the bridesmaids and ushers, walked in, then the bride and her father, Nathan.

The bridesmaids wore pale pink shiffon and satin dresses and carried burnt rose flowers and pale pink peonies. The bride wore an ivory, A-line Victorian lace dress with a scalloped, beaded top. Her train was also scalloped, with beading and lace. Her father wore a black tuxedo, grey vest, and white shirt. Rese was smiling and celebrating his brother's happiness. The colors, the flowers, and the sun beaming through the stained glass windows made the whole processional breathtaking! The mothers lighted the candles, while the song, song "Ave Maria:" Bach/Gounod was played. Aunts recited their assigned Scriptures, and tributes were made to grand-mothers. The preacher delivered a well-received message. The bride and groom said their "I dos." Everyone looked happy and was rejoicing. Carl and I were immensely happy! We were commemorating our son's special occasion.

At the reception, my sisters, brother, nieces, nephews, some of Carl's relatives, his and my friends were all there. Their faces were covered with smiles. We hugged, took pictures, and celebrated together. After a delicious dinner, our son and I danced. I was nervous at first, for I wanted everything to go well on his special day. I remembered stepping on my son's feet in the beginning, but I made up my mind to do the best I could!

Then, it was over, and we could enjoy the rest of the evening. I looked over at Tony as he danced with his wife and shook the hands of the many guests and family members who were present. That was the happiest day of his life, and he deserved every minute of it.

Prayer:

I will praise the name of God with a song
And will magnify Him with thanksgiving.[1]
Lord, God,
Thank You for bringing joy to our hearts.[2]
We had an awesome time
Witnessing our son's matrimony.
You brought Tony and Kate together.[3]
I pray that they would continue to draw
Closer to You, and
That they would live a life of joy
With You at the center of their lives.
In Jesus' name, Amen.

Lord's reply:

"He who finds a wife finds what is good
and receives favor from the Lord."[4]

Reflection:

My family and I had a wonderful time at Tony and Kate's wedding. We were rejoicing and happy. Tony and Kate had made the greatest decision of their lives.

Your reflection:

Did you have occasion to be at your son‘s, daughter‘s, niece‘s, nephew‘s, cousin‘s, sister's or brother's wedding? What were your feelings and experiences?

12

Receiving a Bundle of Joy

The nights rolled on, and the days progressed, nearing the time of the delivery of Kevin, our first and, so far, our only grandchild, who would be born to Tony and Kate. By June 7th 2007, I was already receiving calls from my sisters, who already had lots of grandchildren. They couldn't wait to celebrate with me. Both Tony and Kate had kept me abreast of the progress of the pregnancy, and as I had talked and prayed with Kate on Friday, we had agreed that Kevin was on his way to Mother Earth.

By 11:45 p.m. on Saturday, our son called to tell us that Kate was in labor, and from that moment on, I had difficulty sleeping. I cleaned, did laundry, and, before returning to bed about 3 a.m., I prayed. By early the next afternoon, about 2 p.m., Kate's contractions had increased, and the baby was getting ready for birth. From 2 p.m. until 5:57 p.m., I was becoming uneasy, sensing that something was taking place. A few minutes after 6:00 p.m., I received a call from our son telling me that Kate had given birth to Kevin. He said, "Hi, Mammy, I have great news for you. Kevin is here. You have nothing to worry about; you are now a grandmother, and I am a father."

I was overcome with emotion. "What! I'll be there in a few minutes," I replied. I did not wait to hear the details but quickly got off the phone, related the information to Carl, and was on my way to the hospital. Carl stayed at home with our daughter Jo-An and visited Kate and Kevin the following day.

Kevin was born Sunday, June 9, 2007. He weighed 7 lbs. 9oz., was 19 inches long, and had his first picture taken with him sucking his thumb.

Our son and daughter, Rese and Monique, met me in the waiting room at 7 p.m. We chatted with Tony for a while about the delivery. Tony was doing well, considering what he had gone through the previous hour. We waited for another hour and forty-five minutes before we were able to go to the room to see Kate and Kevin.

As the three of us approached the room, we spotted a nurse tending to a baby just outside Kate's room. Monique ran toward the baby in the tiny bassinet and excitedly said, "Mammy, he is so cute." In that instant, the attending nurse rudely said, "I'm sorry; you are going to have to wait outside until we are finished!" Rese was sleepy from his long day at work, but we encouraged him to stay. We had waited two hours so far, and then waited in the hallway for another half hour, but Kevin was worth the wait. We waited and waited; the half hour wait seemed endless, but it came to an end. The nurse said smilingly, "You can come in now," and in an instant, we rushed into the room.

I said, "Kate, I'm proud of you, girl. I knew you could do it. We are not going to stay too long because we know you had a long and rough day."

She said, "Thanks for your patience, Mother Blake; you heard all the things that Kevin and I went through? Tony, my mother, and I were crying. The baby's shoulder was stuck in the birth canal; I had no strength to push, and Kevin was not breathing when he finally came out. This is another testament to God's goodness, first allowing me to become pregnant, and now, saving our baby's life."

At ten at night, after nineteen hours of labor, Kate still had a beautiful smile on her face. She exhibited courage, strength, and persistence to the end. Tony was ecstatic, smiling, and sending emails and text messages to all his friends. He kept on reminding me, "Mammy, you are a grandmother now, and I am a father."

The next few moments were like finding a jewel in a haystack. First, Monique, with tears running down her cheeks, picked up Kevin and said, "He is so cute!" then offered him to me, then picked him up from my lap, then gave him to Rese.

Rese said, "Nah, I don't want anything to happen to him." I could see a few drops of tears on Rese's face as Monique told him, "You can do it. This is how you hold a baby. Relax your arms, making sure you give the baby head support." Rese held Kevin for about two or three minutes, looking at him closely and enjoying the moment when uncle and nephew came together.

Then, Monique offered the baby to me: "Mammy, do you want to hold him again?"

"Yes," I replied.

I sat down, holding this bundle of joy. I couldn't believe that God could send so much joy into my life. I perused his entire body. He had so much hair, and it was curly too. He had the cutest cheeks, the brightest eyes, the most readable lips; his face was olive in color, but his feet and hands were even lighter. Kevin was alert and ready to achieve greatness at all levels. As I viewed this grandchild from top to bottom, I understood what God was telling me again and again—that nothing was impossible with Him and that Kevin was born with a purpose.

As the days and weeks passed, I had occasion to spend hours with Kevin and his parents. It was a joy for me to change his diaper, feed him, hold him, rock him in my arms, and see his piercing, dark brown eyes as they met mine. I am so grateful to God for giving me the gift of being a grandmother. I will cherish this gift as long as I live. Kevin recently celebrated his first birthday.

Prayer:

Praise God from whom all blessings come.[1]
Lord, thank You for Your protection
And care for both Kate and Kevin
During Kevin's delivery.[2]
I pray that as Kevin grows up to boyhood and
Manhood,
That You would continue to watch over his life
And protect him.
I pray, Lord, that You would birth greatness in Kevin,
And that you would use him for Your glory.
In Jesus' name, I pray, Amen.

The Lord's reply:

"Yes, I have loved [him] with
an everlasting love;
Therefore with loving kindness
I have drawn [him]."[3]

Reflection:

As I sat and held Kevin, I sensed that he was in God's hands. He would be a warrior for God; one who would not be afraid to speak and stand up for God.

Your reflection:

Did you have a son, daughter, stepchild, grandchild, a nephew, niece, or cousin born recently or in the past? Begin to pray for him or her. Write down what you want God to do in his or her life.

13

Taking Vacations

For me, a vacation meant a change of pace, a change of scenery, and a time of refreshing with my family. Vacations with our children, included family camping in Maine and short trips to the Cape Islands. Carl accompanied us when he was not busy at work. He preferred vacations on the island of Trinidad with extended family members and, on occasion, with our sons and daughter. International travel for six people, for me, was complex and costly. I loved the simplicity of our Maine and Cape vacations, the opportunity to leave house duties behind, enjoy myself, and bond with our family without traveling too far. I hated flying!

Cabins in the Maine camp were rugged and bathrooms and showers were centrally located, making it difficult during the night, when my children and I needed to use the bathroom. However, I loved family camping, because it was affordable and included breakfast, lunch, and dinner. Staff activities with the children in the morning and at night allowed me to have time for group activities with other adults or simply afforded me time to rest or go to the movies. After lunch, our children and I would spend quality time at the beach, amusement parks, and shopping with camp staff.

In July, 1983, I was reminiscing about the beauty of Maine amid the pain that I was experiencing from swollen legs, for I was in my seventh month of pregnancy with our daughter, Jo-An. I knew that, even with the pain of swollen legs, I was prepared to make the best of our vacation, remaining strong for our children who depended on me to show them a good time. Thinking how I could manage alone with our three children, I heard the camp counselor call for them to go to their respective groups.

"Oh, what a great feeling," I thought. "The children will stay busy making various crafts for a whole morning, and I can attend an adult Bible study or have quiet time." I decided to attend the Bible study.

The Bible study discussion was on 1 Corinthians 13, the love chapter. God teaches us the importance of genuinely loving one another. Each one of us had something to say about his or her struggles with love in the body of Christ, in our homes, and with our neighbors. It was time for me to respond! But in a split second, we heard a sound, and a staff member barged into the room and asked permission to speak to me, and of course, I walked out of the room. I knew something was wrong! My boys had done it again. They were misbehaving! I learned that they had taken a bike, belonging to the camp, from another child and had refused to return it. Their refusal caused a scuffle, and there it was—total embarrassment for me, even in my peaceful time.

"I have never experienced this problem in this family camp before! " I said.

Everyone looked at me as I walked out the door. Weren't we just discussing love? Yet, no one appeared ready to apply LOVE or to show compassion toward me. I experienced self-pity and rejection as I questioned why no one understood my feeling lonely, empty, and out of control. Frustration and confusion welled up inside me as I was there alone with our three children.

"Why couldn't our sons behave so that I could have a chance to rest and enjoy the beautiful morning?" I thought.

The answer came back: "What is worse, staying home with your children and not going anywhere, or taking chances and still having fun?"

Recognizing that there was some truth in what I was thinking, I pictured the beautiful ocean and the wonderful time we would have at the beach that afternoon. The camp counselor told my boys to give up the bike. When I got into our cabin, I told the boys, "I want you Rese and Tony to behave yourselves in this camp, you hear me! We are on vacation and I am not going to tolerate anything less. Do you understand?"

"Yes, Mammy," they replied.

We had lunch that afternoon in the great dining hall. The children got a chance to see and be with people of diverse backgrounds and challenges and yes, it got better in the afternoon when we went to the beach as a family. People gave me rides to and from the beach, and I really felt that their kindness was a sign of God's love for me. After dinner, Rese and Monique sang a duet. The good outweighed the bad. God gave me patience and hope during that difficult morning.

Although we stayed in a hotel, our trips to the Cape were not as much fun as our Maine trips. We had fun swimming in the hotel's pool, shopping, and eating out. On one occasion, our sons, Tony and Rese, had a scuffle as they were exiting out of the car and Rese accidently broke his nose. The children and I spent hours in the emergency room, sad for Rese, but disappointed that his accident ruined our vacation. I decided that I would take only our daughters on future vacations to Maine or the Cape, while my husband would take our sons on vacation to Trinidad.

As our children got older, we rented motels in Maine which afforded us greater amenities such as a bathroom in the room, a small refrigerator to store milk and juice, an inside swimming pool, sauna, and whirlpool. For breakfast, lunch, and dinner, we would drive to seafood and fast-food restaurants. We had fun bowling and shopping.

Our daughters, Monique and Jo-An, accompanied me on my trip to Trinidad in January, 1995. We nearly missed the flight from Miami Airport because of the time it took for us to change to another plane. Our worst nightmare on our arrival in Trinidad, was finding out that our luggage was not present, and that we would have to wait for at least two days. That thought was unnerving.

We spent most of our ten-day trip visiting and having dinner with relatives and friends, having picnics at the beaches and at Maracas Waterfalls while enjoying the birds and the beautiful butterflies, visiting Point-a-Pierre Wild Forest Museum, eating out at Chinese and other restaurants, touring the oil fields, and attending church services at different venues. It was just wonderful to simply walk in the blazing hot sun. It brought back childhood memories.

In my growing up years in Trinidad, I had never had such fun. My parents had encouraged me to work extremely hard in school and to be diligent about my spiritual life. I missed the opportunity and enjoyment of mountain climbing and wasn't sure that I could climb a mountain. My first response when asked to climb by my children was, "I can't climb all the way up there. Are you kidding?"

"Mammy, you can do it. Don't look at the height; just put your feet in each cleft; you can do it," they told me.

"Ok, I am going to do this. I am going to overcome this hurdle. I have made up my mind," I thought to myself.

And so, step by step, I walked up, and up, higher and higher. I could not believe that I had accomplished what I had set out to do. It was so beautiful to sit and have a picnic lunch and view the waterfalls. What I liked the most was the sight of a beautiful butterfly, which landed right before me with colors of bright splendor. It was not that I had never seen a butterfly, but I had never had the time to pay attention to the beauty and the array of colors it contained.

As I reminisced about my time in Trinidad, I could not help but praise God for his greatness and pray concerning my loneliness and what I had communicated with God about on that summer day in July, 1983, pregnant with Jo-An.

Prayer:

I will praise You, the Lord, with all of my being.

With my lips, I will sing praises unto You.[1]

Lord, I confess my feelings of emptiness and loneliness.

I repent and ask Your forgiveness for these sins.

Thank You for always being there for me.[2]

Lord, only You know the reason for my emptiness.[3]

I feel empty from deep within as

I continue to experience burdens.

I pray, Lord, that You would soothe and
Comfort me in my loneliness,
That I do not feel like giving up.
Lord, please heal my lonely heart and set me free.
In Jesus' name, I pray, Amen.

The Lord's reply:

"I, even I, am He who comforts you.
Who are you that you fear mortal men,
the sons of men, who are but grass,
that you forget the Lord your Maker,
who stretched out the heavens
and laid the foundation of the earth?" [4]

Reflection:

I learned so much from that experience. The fact that the day didn't start off on a good note was not an occasion for me to feel sad and gloomy. All things work together for good,[5] and it is good to thank God in all circumstances.[6] I did not have to feel embarrassed. Naturally, parents go through trying times with their children. I assumed that the staff did not exhibit love toward me, but I was judging them because I was feeling badly about myself. We should always be mindful of what we say or how we act. It is best to remain calm in the midst of a crisis. If not, the tendency is for us to be defensive, blurt out and say what we do not mean to say, which is what I did. I was certainly not expressing love.

Your reflection:

What were your experiences during family vacations or reunions? What did you learn during those important times?

14

Going on My Getaways

My getaways were the times I retreated to the Cape to be in the presence of God, to hear from Him, and to evaluate myself as a child of God, a wife, and a mother. It was a time to be revived, to be renewed, and to recognize where God was taking me in my life. Carl was very supportive of me, taking time from work to care for the children and doing the best he could with house-hold chores.

I visited the Cape at least once per year for a two-day retreat at a local hotel. When I would get to the hotel room, the first thing I would do would be to go under the covers. Not having to prepare a meal or do dishes and laundry or speak to another adult was comforting. My going under the covers was a symbol of rest and security with God. I could talk to Him in the peace and quietness of my surroundings without interruption, anxiety, or distractions. I would engross myself in prayer, study His Word, listen to His voice, and write in my journal. That time was special to me, because at home, I didn't have time to do those important things; I was diligent in prayer but not disciplined in studying God's Word.

During my retreats, I recorded my love for the Lord and how much I needed to be changed. I expressed my weariness, my brokenness, my anxieties, my fears, and how I needed God to fix some things in my life. I continued to bathe myself in God's love and spent quality time with Him, staying up for hours reading and writing. During the morning hours, I would do some walking, and in the evening, I would have a delicious meal, sit in the sauna for a bit, and revert to the covers again.

My getaways were not only long trips. I also used every opportunity to get out of the house. I would go to the library for hours either on Thursday or Saturday to read and write, or visit my natural food store to buy nutritional foods. I felt rejuvenated each time I took such small breaks.

One weekend in June, 1999, my childhood friend invited me to hear her preach in Louisiana at a small country church. She was staying at the home of one of the women from the church who gladly welcomed me at her home, which was in a private, wooded area owned by this woman and her family.

The morning of the conference, I took a walk to commune with God. I felt the need to completely surrender everything to God—my household, my life, my job, all that I owned. God was showing me how to love others, even when I was not loved, that love was the tool that I needed in my life to overcome barriers and difficulties. God wanted my attention, and, most of all, He desired my obedience.

The message at the conference later that day was, "Sitting at the Feet of Jesus and Listening." The Gospel of Luke records two sisters, Mary and Martha, who were in the company of Jesus. Martha was busy preparing the house, cleaning, and cooking, while Mary was sitting at the feet of Jesus, listening and receiving from Jesus, learning about Him, and getting to know Him intimately.

"But Martha was distracted with much serving, and she approached Him and said, 'Lord, do you not care that my sister has left me to serve alone? Therefore tell her to help me' " (Luke 10:40 NKJV).

"And Jesus answered and said to her, 'Martha, Martha, you are worried and troubled about many things. But one thing is needed, and Mary has chosen that good part, which will not be taken away from her' " (Luke 10:41-42 NKJV).

Often, we are so busy doing ministry that we forget to sit, hear, and learn what, where, and how Jesus wants us to conduct the ministry that will glorify HIM.

In 2003, I attended a conference in Vermont, and the message taken from Hebrews 6 and Mark 5, was entitled, "Blessed to Be a Blessing." The speaker summarized her message by saying, "Jesus Christ answers desperate cries, even those of the demonic man who was in bondage and lived in utter loneliness, torment, deeply scarred, and rejected." She continued, "Only Jesus could subdue him. Human eyes could not see the potential in the man of 'The Gadarenes,' but God did. God gave him an "inheritance of glory, a passion for hearts, a birthing of revival." The Lord, the king of glory, reaches and helps us in our darkness and in our loneliness. God heals us when we are at our worst, and He uses the least of us.

Prayer:

Wonderful Savior, Wonderful Lord![1]
I praise You this morning.
I confess my sin of
Busyness that has kept me from
Listening to You, Lord.
I repent of my busyness.
Please forgive me Lord, for my sin.
Thank You for standing and knocking
At the door of my heart.[2]
I pray, Lord, that You would answer my
Desperate cries and deliver me.
In Jesus' name, I pray, Amen.

The Lord's reply:

"Come to me, all you who are weary and burdened, and I will give you rest. Take my yoke upon you and learn from me, for I am gentle and humble in heart, and you will find rest for your souls. For my yoke is easy and my burden is light."[3]

Reflection:

God's voice is a soft whisper of love which we sometimes fail to hear.

Your reflection:

Describe your getaway—your sanctuary where you and God meet. Describe areas in your life where God has delighted to make changes. In what ways have you grown through your daily walk with the Lord?

15

Experiencing Anxieties

In 1991, during the time that I operated a home-based consulting business, I worried about whether my business would be sufficient for our daily upkeep and whether it would bring in enough income to fund our children's higher education. I wondered whether, if I resorted to a full-time job to satisfy those needs, that job would afford me the time that I needed to work in ministry.

Anxieties plagued my mind. Where was I? Where was I headed? How was I feeling? I was giving my entire self to my family and not doing enough for me. I was drowning in the midst of despair, forgetting to save myself while preserving others. I was forever busy, assisting our children in their various activities: homework, extracurricular activities, or their needs in general. I was listening, loving, and advocating for them. While I was busy being a mother, I felt I was forgetting about myself.

I could not solve those problems by myself. I resorted to my journals often, jotting down how I felt a certain day and turning over my thoughts to someone Who was bigger than me, One who could bear my problems and guide me accordingly. I prayed.

Prayer:

Everlasting Father, our hope in the time of need,[1]
My rock, my fortress, and my deliverer,[2]
I confess my sin of anxiety and my
Failure to release my burdens to You.
I repent of my sin of anxiety.
Forgive me for being anxious, Lord.
Thank You for hearing my prayers.[3]
I continue to face anxieties: sinking in financial debt;
Being weary from house duties; working at my job;
And raising four children.
I feel that I am giving up my whole life for
The sake of my family and losing my self-worth.
I now pray, Father that You would lift my burdens.
Help me to rest and depend on You.
In Jesus' name, Amen.

The Lord's reply:

"Do not be anxious about anything, but in everything, by prayer and petition, with thanksgiving, present your requests to God. And the peace of God, which transcends all understanding, will guard your hearts and your minds in Christ Jesus."[4]

Reflection:

Life is not promised to anyone. One should spend quality time with one's family. In times of trial, we should make a mental note of how good God has been to us and change from complaining to thanksgiving.

Your reflection:

Reflect on areas in your life that cause you anxiety. Confess these anxieties to God. Pray and ask God to increase your faith.

16

Experiencing Fear of Fear

No amount of activities, trips, or joy could erase the thoughts that entered my mind from time to time. I experienced fear of fear: fear that my children may get sick, fear that I may die and my children would not have anyone to take care of them the way I did, and fear of financial bondage. The list went on. I was not surrendering my life to God, but felt instead, that I was responsible for my children's, my husband's, and my success.

I experienced such fear on one of my getaways to the Berkshires to hear the Boston Pops. I took a bus and a taxi and stayed at a large Victorian home that was a bed and breakfast. The owner of the home promised that she would give me a ride to the concert, but at the last minute, she changed her mind and arranged for her male guest, who was also attending the concert, to give me a ride there. I reluctantly accepted.

On our way to the concert, John was not too talkative. His sunken eyes and quiet appearance scared me. I knew that after the show, I should return with someone else, but I had no one to give me a ride. As the show came to a close, I began to feel uneasy, afraid, and desperate. I approached a female usher after the concert and said, "Ma'am, I am in dire need of a ride to where I am staying. I do not feel safe with the person who accompanied me here, and I am afraid that something awful may happen to me; could you please help me?"

"Let me see what I can do," she replied.

With that said, she went off in a different direction, and I had to walk as fast as I could to catch up with her. When I caught up with her, she explained that the person, whom she had thought of, did not have room in her car.

With heart pounding, I approached the ticket attendant and asked, "Sir, is it possible for me to call a taxi? I need to leave immediately, because I do not feel safe returning with the man who dropped me off earlier." The ticket attendant understood my plight.

He said, "A taxi is on its way to pick up a few folks; why don't you wait here until the taxi comes and share the cost with those people?" When the taxi came, I ran hastily into it, hoping to get to the house before John. But the taxi driver was obligated to drop off two people first before dropping me off. That took time. Finally, the driver got to the house and waited for me to get in, but John had driven up at the same time. I realized that the owner was out, since her car was not there.

I got out of the taxi, walked up to the house, and entered. My heart was thumping. I sat in the first chair that I could find and, trying to maintain my composure, started a conversation.

"Wasn't that a great concert?"

"Yes, it was."

He continued, "Is this your first time to the Berkshires?"

I answered, "Yes, I always had a desire to come to Tanglewood since I was in college."

"Oh, that is wonderful."

"Gee, I am getting tired," I said.

"Me, too," he said.

I began to think, "Lord, I am trapped in this large house with a strange man. Only you can protect me now." (My knees buckled at this moment.) I had read about horrible things that happened to women. Would I make the Sunday morning news? I thought of the headline: *The family of Joan M. Blake is offering a reward for anyone who has information concerning her. She was last seen boarding a bus to the Berkshires to attend a Tanglewood concert.*

At that very moment, the owner of the house drove up and entered the living room where we were.

"How did you both enjoy the concert?"

"I really did, but it was so difficult to get transportation back to the house."

"I thought John was bringing you back."

"I guess we missed each other because of the crowd. Anyway, I think I am going to bed now."

"Joan, you already know where your room is. John's room is next to yours."

I went upstairs to my room and locked my door securely, but fear grasped me for the entire night. I could feel my heart thumping. I got up several times and listened close to the door, certain that I heard footsteps in the hallway, or was that a figment of my own imagination? I couldn't tell, and I wasn't going to try to find out, either. I read a few verses from Psalm 91 and Psalm 139. I began to write a letter to the owner. The following are excerpts from the letter:

Dear Jane,

You are a wonderful person, and you have a beautiful home. Thank you for making it possible for me to come to Tanglewood.

As you know, we can't always trust strangers. You were so kind to arrange a ride for me with John. However, it did not quite work out. I took a taxi back to the house and was petrified, even though the taxi driver waited until I got inside.

I did not feel comfortable with John or feel comfortable with him on the same floor as I was. I was frightened the entire night as I thought I heard someone turning my door knob. I guess the bed and breakfast was just not for me.

I continued writing the letter and thought of giving the owner the letter the next morning but thought to myself, "But what difference would that make?" I was leaving in the morning. No one cared how I felt. I was afraid to leave my room in the middle of the night, although the bathroom was across from my room. All I could remember was that John's room was next to mine. Would I ever fall asleep? Just then, I thought of praying, and I don't remember anything else after that. . .

Prayer:

Magnificent God, King of Kings and Lord of Lords,[1]
You are magnificent in the heavens.
I magnify Your name, God.[2]

Experiencing Fear of Fear

I confess that I feel tormented by constant fears.
I repent of my fears.
And ask forgiveness for my sins.
Thank You that You are my God.[3]
I pray that You would rid me of fear, in Jesus' name.
Please protect me during the night
From any evil that is lurking against me.
Assure me of Your presence[4] Lord,
And give me the confidence that I need
To face my fears.
Lord, I pray that I would wake up,
Leave this place, and
Safely return home to my family.
In Jesus' name, Amen.

The Lord's reply:

"Fear not, for I have redeemed you;
I have summoned you by name; you are mine.
When you pass through the waters,
I will be with you;
and when you pass through the rivers,
they will not sweep over you.
When you walk through the fire,
you will not be burned;
the flames will not set you ablaze."[5]

Reflection:

One cannot experience fear and proclaim faith simultaneously. As we ask God to remove the fear from our lives, we begin to build faith. Till this day, I don't know what I was hearing during the night, whether they were footsteps or the sounds from the house itself. I am reminded by that experience to stay in a hotel or a motel, where there are lots of people or to be in the company of friends if I stay at a bed and breakfast.

Your reflection:

What are you afraid of? Why are you afraid? Confess your fears. Ask God to increase your faith.

17

Experiencing Fear of Sickness

When our children hurt themselves, I didn't take it lightly. I cried when a nail got into Monique's foot, and when Monique accidentally caused Jo-An to fall. I cried myself to sleep when Rese fell off a table at a daycare he was attending and his eyes were swollen for days. I cried when I accidentally slammed the door on Jo-An's finger when she was about four years old and really believed that I had cut off her finger. Carl and I were waiting in the emergency room for most of the night, and I spent time worrying about our daughter's finger, which ended up being okay. I don't remember Carl ever getting sick except for when he had chicken pox. He remained strong and supportive of our family, even more so when the children were sick.

I remember times when I was ill and times when I even had to undergo surgery. Because of my past experiences, I was afraid of ever being ill.

One day during my personal Bible reading, I had a panic attack that made me feel like I was dying. I called my sister, who sent her husband to help me. I opened every window so I could breathe. I had a similar episode on another occasion. I ran outside and knocked on my neighbor's door, but there was no one there. I ran back inside, loosened my clothes, drank a hot cup of tea, and began to pray. I was sure I wouldn't be alive when my husband came home. I sat and thought about where my children would be if I were to die. Already, they depended on me for moral support, for nurturing and caring for them, for being their advocate at school, and for showing them a good time. Moreover, I loved to show them how great God is and how God is the One they should thank for making a way for them.

Three months after giving birth to Jo-An, in December, 1983, my husband Carl had gone to Trinidad to visit his mother and, lo and behold, I ended up in an emergency ward and had to undergo surgery. The presence of an infection delayed my surgery for an additional two weeks. I was disappointed that I could not continue to breast feed my baby Jo-An. My aunt-in-law, Gracie, now deceased, stayed at our home and cared for the children until Carl's return two days following my hospital admission.

During my hospital stay, our former pastor came to the hospital several times to pray with me. He introduced me to Psalm 121, which to this day has blessed me and given me hope. Psalm 121 states, "I lift my eyes to the hills—where does my help come from? My help comes from the Lord, the Maker of heaven and earth" (NIV). I will never forget the love and kindness that I received from this former pastor and church members. They prepared meals and took turns cleaning our home and caring for our children. The doctors were kind but firm, sending me home on Christmas Day for a brief visit and postponing surgery until after Christmas.

When they told me I could go home for a few hours on Christmas

Day, I felt I was coming to the end of my rope. Is this how dying feels? One sees one's family for a few hours and feels lucky that one has that time? I knew I was not dying, but I took that time seriously. I was grieving from my separation from Jo-An, our new baby. I knew God would take care of me, but fear still gripped my soul as I spoke to God concerning my upcoming surgery and asked for healing then and at other times. His words of love and faithfulness soothed my aching heart.

Prayer

Merciful God, Mighty God,[1]
You are the great I AM.[2]
I love You, Lord and Savior;
I love You because You first loved me.[3]
I confess my fear of sickness, and, Lord, I
Repent of this sin.
Please forgive me, Lord.
I know for certain that You sacrificed Yourself
For my salvation.[4]
Thanks for blessing me with a wonderful family.
I am experiencing panic attacks
And fear of getting sick again.
I pray, Lord, that You would extend my life,
And give me the opportunity to see my children grow.
I pray Lord, that You would see me through this difficult surgery
That I can be with my family.

In Jesus' name, Amen.

The Lord's reply:

"There is no fear in love; but perfect love casts out fear, because fear involves torment. But he who fears has not been made perfect in love."[5]

Reflection:

God allowed those illnesses to remind me of how precious every moment is. Not only are we to use our time wisely and do God's will, but, also, we are to love our family members. I was excited to be able to go home after my surgeries to spend precious moments with my family. God used those and other difficult experiences to show me that He is in control of my life and that I can trust Him even in the big things.

Your reflection:

Reflect on your fear of sickness. Confess this fear to God. Read Scriptures that deal with healing, and, if you are sick, profess your faith that you will be healed in the name of Christ.

18

Having Friends

My husband's friends were his childhood friends from Trinidad who visited him annually for Christmas celebrations or who dropped in from time to time, while my friends were from former churches and from the residence where I stayed the first year I came to America.

Four of my friends and I were part of a support group from a former church. We met consistently as a support group for two years to keep in touch and to lend support to one another. When we met and discussed our pain, our struggles, and our family issues, we knew that we could count on one another to listen, to comfort, to strengthen, and to encourage. While in our support group, I once expressed my struggle with keeping up with housework while pregnant with Jo-An, and the women came to my assistance. They painted our living room, one did a load of laundry and made me a maternity blouse, and another cooked a meal. Another accompanied me to my pregnancy classes, came to the hospital at 4 a.m., stayed with me during labor, and witnessed Jo-An's birth.

We five did not have everything in common. In fact, each person was unique and had different goals and viewpoints, yet, we were committed to our friendships. One friend from the group moved away, and some of us had a chance to visit with her at her home or on her visits to Boston. However, we four still meet three or four times per year for breakfast or lunch; we exchange presents and talk about our current issues and those in our families. We attended baby showers, christenings, weddings, wedding anniversaries, cookouts, graduations, and the funeral services of loved ones.

There were other friends from this former church who visited us from time to time and reached out by inviting Carl and me to their homes during the summer and Christmas seasons. We were also friends with a couple whose daughter and Jo-An became friends at school and attended each other's birthday parties. It seemed that every time I had car failure after dropping Jo-An off at school, I would get help from this family. Getting help was not the key to our friendship, however. The fact that we could support each other in good times and in bad made our friendship strong. When we met at their home, our home, or the YMCA, we prayed for and supported one another.

Then there was my very good friend and others from the residence who would meet with me for lunch occasionally. This dear friend is the godmother of our daughter, Monique. Recently, she celebrated her birthday at a restaurant in Boston and invited Monique, and eight of us, some of whom had lived at the residence, to participate in her birthday celebration. She treated us to a lavish tea and a harpist entertained us. We reviewed our past pictures, took new ones, and reminisced about the times we had together.

Having Friends

I have friends whom I met at conferences and came to know quite well. I have had occasion to spend time in their homes and to attend their churches. They mean so much to me because we are bonded by the love of God and are transparent to one another. When we hurt, we share what is on our minds.

I gained friends from my current church and from seminary, friends at our local YMCA, friendly neighbors, friends who would pray for and with me, friends who would say a good word to encourage me, friends whom I just didn't know I had, ones God put in my path for me to bless and from whom I could receive a blessing.

Prayer:

I bow before You and worship You, Lord,
God of Hosts.[1]
I confess and repent of ill thoughts that
I may have against my friends.
Please forgive me for my sins, Lord.
Thank You for being my friend[2]
And sending good friends into my life.
Lord, I pray for friends everywhere,
Friends whom I have known for a long time,
And those whom You are about to put in my path.
I pray that as friends we would continue to be supportive,
Real, and there for one another.
In Jesus' name, Amen.

The Lord's reply:

"This is My commandment,
that you love one another as I have
loved you.
Greater love has no one than
this, than to lay down one's life for
his friends."[3]

Reflection:

Friendship is mutual. It's a time of sharing, learning, supporting, and growing. Good friends are dear and are to be cherished.

Your reflection:

Reflect on friends who have been good to you. Do you have friends who are struggling? Reach out and be compassionate to that person who needs you.

19

Dealing with Anger

By 1990, I was worn out by overwhelming household duties. My husband, who is a great provider, supported our children particularly with their extra-curricular activities. He would often help with grocery shopping and laundry and make small repairs around the house. Yet, I felt there was always so much for me to do.

Pain and joy were woven into the fabric of my life. On the one hand, I felt joy being a wife and mother, but on the other hand, I felt the burdens of extended family members and issues in our own household. I felt lonely during those times and thought that being involved in our children's lives would take away the void, but it did not. I had become everything to everyone, slowly getting myself into a rut, masking the pain and anger, emotions that lay dormant while I continued to live under a façade. I was not receiving enough help in our household; dishes were piling up while my life seemingly was tumbling down. I did not have time to read or write; the things I liked to do best. This led to a feeling of anger and resentment, and I asked God to forgive me of my sins and to give me a heart of love, joy, and peace. The process of forgiveness and reconciliation was not easy for me. I handled anger by not relating well to people with whom I had problems.

I continued to give God my laundry list of prayers for our family's needs and those of others. For example, I prayed for help in making decisions regarding school placements for Jo-An, then seven years old, for God to cleanse my heart, to give me patience and humility in my marriage, to provide financial relief, to increase my business so it would glorify Him, to give me wisdom, to help me enjoy and be engrossed in His Word, to guide and strengthen me, to heal my body, to improve my relationships—It was a list that seemed to have no end, and I was praying, praying, praying but simply wanting my own way and could not perceive that God was pointing me in another direction. Then there were days that I just simply thanked God for being my Counselor, for opening the door for Him and I to sup together, for allowing me to learn from Him and about Him, for being with me through the valleys and mountainous journeys over the years, for providing for me, for using the valleys to increase my faith and trust in Him, for being a God Who was truly wise, faithful, loving, forgiving, and compassionate.[1]

But my anger and resentment never seemed to go away, leaving me with no control over what was happening to me, or over the circumstances I was experiencing in and out of my household. Thoughts continued to bottle up within me, causing me pain, frustration, and even illness. So, I turned to God in prayer.

Prayer:

I praise You, Lord God of Heaven and Earth.[2]
For You said praise is comely for the
Righteous.[3]
I confess all my feelings of anger, resentment,
And bitterness.
I repent of these sins, Lord.
Please forgive me for sinning against You.
Thank You, Lord, for loving me.[4]
I pray that you would deliver me from
Anger, resentment, and bitterness.
In Jesus' name, Amen.

The Lord's reply:

"Get rid of all bitterness, rage and anger, brawling and slander, along with every form of malice. Be kind and compassionate to one another, forgiving each other, just as in Christ God forgave you."[5]

Reflection:

Holding on to anger, resentment, and bitterness for a season robbed me of an awesome relationship with Almighty God through His Son, Jesus. People who made me angry didn't know or care if I was angry. I was only hurting myself in the process.

Your reflection:

Reflect on a time in your life when you were angry with someone. If you are still angry, confess your anger to God. Ask God for forgiveness. Take steps to rectify your anger.

20

Dealing with Guilt

From an early age, I was plagued with guilt. Somehow, I felt that I should be grateful for everything that my mother and father had done for me. My mother would discuss other young women who did not make their parents happy, and I knew what she expected of me.

I felt guilty when my mother and father asked me whom I loved more. I loved my father more, but I couldn't hurt my mother's feelings, so from a child, I was put in a position to please others rather than be open and honest about the way I felt. That position continually robbed me of who I really was, of what I wanted to attain, and of how I was to reach my destiny. When I wasn't honest with myself and instead, did the things I thought were important to others, I became a people pleaser and did what people wanted me to do. When I made decisions on important issues, I still sought affirmation from others.

Guilt became a part of my life and walked with me throughout my life. I felt guilty when the phone rang, so although I was busy, I would spend time speaking to a friend or a relative, who, by the way, happened to have a cordless phone and could do their chores while I stayed glued to my phone and got nothing done. I was hurting their feelings if I said, "Could I call you back?" Worse yet, if I was packing my bag to go to the gym and a son or daughter called while en route to their jobs, I would feel guilty, so I would pick up the telephone instead of walking right out the door. I would waste forty-five minutes of my gym time when I could have called them later.

If I couldn't attend a church or family related event to which I was invited, I was disappointing someone, so I changed that by being everywhere at all times. When the house was not clean, the dishes weren't washed, or dinner was not prepared, I felt guilty for not pleasing my husband so I did them all. Being honest and telling him what was on my mind would have led to hurt feelings and subsequent arguments, so I kept things to myself and became angry. Guilt kept me in bondage.

When I went on my getaways and didn't take our children with me, I felt like I was abandoning them so nearing the end of my stay, I would invite our two daughters to stay the last night. When I sat down to read a good book and there was something else to do, guilt stepped in, so I did what was needed. Guilt followed me when I went shopping for myself, so I would purchase items for my family instead. I felt I should not spend too much on new furniture, so I invested in used ones. These were some of the areas in which guilt played a major role. Today, my life has improved a little in this area, but I continue to pray and to ask God to rid me of guilt.

Prayer:

Majesty, how much I love You today!
I confess the sin of guilt, and, Father,
I repent of this sin.
Please forgive me, Lord, for my guilt.
Thank You that You sent Your only Son to show us
By example how we should live.[1]
I pray that You would deliver me from guilt.
In Jesus' name, Amen.

The Lord's reply:

"It is for freedom that Christ has set [you] free. Stand firm, then, and do not let yourselves be burdened again by a yoke of slavery."[2]

Reflection:

Although I have come a long way, I am still dealing with guilt. If I have to read or write, I go to the library to avoid feeling guilty for spending time alone and not tending to everyone else.

Your reflection:

Think about a period in your life when you suffered from guilt. What caused you to feel guilty? Begin to make a mental note or an actual list about areas in your life where guilt is apparent. Confess, repent, and ask God's forgiveness for the guilt you have harbored so long. Begin putting your plans for dealing with guilt, into action, when you see guilt approaching.

21

Dealing with Un-forgiveness

This journey of submerging in and experiencing God's love took place particularly during my retreats on the Cape. I had so much to tell God, so much to deal with, so much to ask forgiveness for, but the two or three nights would pass by so quickly that before long, I would return to the busyness of my life again and forget that God had met me there.

My feeling of resentment had become a part of my life now. What had started as a small seed was growing and finding root. I tried to go away on retreats, thinking that I needed rest, but it was my unforgiving heart that kept me running away. I was running away from myself and refusing to deal with the issue. But as I kept going to God in my time alone, God kept pointing me to my unforgiving heart toward others.

The more I thought about the person who had said something about me or had done me wrong, the longer I failed to forgive him or her for the wrong he or she had done. It was difficult for me to forgive someone because I viewed that person as needing to be punished for the wrong he or she had committed. Forgiving that person, I thought, was letting him or her off the hook. What I didn't know was that un-forgiveness was destroying my relationship with God. When I had gone to a family member and reinstated our friendship, I would become angry all over again for the failure of that family member to talk about the issue completely or to ask forgiveness concerning the matter. I finally realized that I was taking matters into my own hands by analyzing how the issue should be resolved, rather than leaving the matter to God.

I faced the issue of pride when I followed God's leading to forgive. In order to forgive, I had to relinquish pride; forgive the person, and love him or her. God has allowed me to see the good in a person through the eyes of Christ. In the past, I have taken the hurtful things that people said to me as personal and I have allowed myself to harbor un-forgiveness. Disregarding the hurt is so difficult for me, but in those situations, I pray to God and ask Him to heal my unforgiving heart.

Prayer:

All praises go to You, Mighty King,[1]
Enthroned in the Heavens![2]
Lord, I confess my sin of un-forgiveness.
I repent and ask You, Lord, to please
Forgive me for my sin.
Father, thank You for working continually
In my life.[3]
I pray, Lord, that I would walk in love, and

Forgive others even when
They have wronged me.
I pray this in Jesus' name, Amen.

The Lord's reply:

"For if you forgive men when they sin against you, your heavenly Father will also forgive you. But if you do not forgive men their sins, your Father will not forgive your sins."[4]

Reflection:

Our actions should flow from our willingness to obey the Holy Spirit. They should not be based on our feelings.

Your reflection:

Reflect on your past hurt. If you have been unforgiving to a person who has hurt you, confess this to God and ask for His forgiveness. If possible, make restitution between you and the person who has hurt you.

22

Learning Nutrition

I understood the importance of good nutrition much later in life, particularly when I was faced with frequent illnesses. The following is a brief summary of what our body needs and the reason for my desiring to get this knowledge. The four basic nutrients are water, carbohydrates, proteins, and fats, and they are the basic building blocks of a good diet.[1]

Our body is two-thirds water. Water is essential for transporting nutrients and waste products in and out of cells and for maintaining proper body temperature. It is suggested that one drinks eight 8-ounce glasses of water a day to ensure proper health.[2]

Carbohydrates supply the body with the energy it needs to function. They are derived from fruits, vegetables, peas and beans, milk and milk products. Carbohydrates are divided into two kinds: simple and complex. Fruits are one of the richest natural sources of simple carbohydrates. Complex carbohydrates include fiber and starches, such as vegetables, whole grains, peas, and beans. Carbohydrates are the main source of blood glucose, which is a major fuel for all of the body's cells and the only source of energy for the brain and red blood cells. It is suggested that one consumes natural foods rather than refined or processed foods. Refined foods, such as soft drinks, cakes, and candy are loaded with sugar and are detrimental to good health. A high fiber diet helps to prevent constipation and reduces the risk of colon cancer.[3]

Protein is important for growth and development. As a provider of energy for the body, it is necessary for the manufacture of hormones, antibodies, enzymes, and tissues. The body makes amino acids when it recognizes the various intake of foods, for example, complete proteins like meat, fish, eggs, cheese, poultry, and the incomplete proteins found in whole grains, legumes, and leafy green vegetables.[4] My herbalist suggested that I stay away from red meat. Other health professionals believe that, because antibiotics and chemicals are used in growing livestock and poultry, dairy products present a high health risk.[5] It is important, then, to use substitutes, including beans, nuts, and seeds, in one's diet, because they are filled with proteins.

During infancy and childhood, our bodies needed fat for normal brain development. Fat is the most concentrated source of energy available to the body.[6] As we grow older, we should be mindful of the foods that we eat, since those can turn into various fats, such as saturated fats, polyunsaturated fats, monounsaturated fats, and trans-fatty acids.

Saturated fatty acids are found in animal products, in dairy products as well as some vegetable products such as beef and pork, whole milk, cream, cheese, as well as coconut oil, palm kernel oil, and vegetable shortening. Since the liver uses saturated fats to manufacture cholesterol, a high intake of saturated fats can lead to high cholesterol levels.

Polyunsaturated fatty acids are found in corn, soybean, safflower, sunflower oils, and certain fish oils. These oils tend to lower blood cholesterol levels. Research has shown that a high intake of these acids can reduce your good cholesterol.

Monounsaturated fatty acids are found mostly in vegetable and nut oils, such as olive, peanut, and canola. These oils tend to lower blood cholesterol without affecting the good cholesterol.

Trans-fatty acids exist in processed and hardened vegetable oils. Examples of these kinds of oils include margarine and shortening. Studies have shown that these fatty acids behave like saturated fatty acids by increasing blood cholesterol levels.[7]

I understand now why my mother placed so much importance on nutrition. A typical breakfast in our family consisted of porridge, which could either be sago (resembles quinoa), barley or cornmeal, eggs, cheese, and toast, which provided us with complex carbohydrates, major energy fuel, fiber, and protein for us kids.

Our lunch, which was filled with complex carbohydrates, included rice, leafy and root vegetables, legumes, meat, fish and fruit. Leafy and root vegetables consisted of bukchoy, green cabbage, callaloo (made from spinach), carrots, sweet potatoes, yams, plantains, dasheen, edoes, and cassava. Legumes included lentil peas, red beans, pigeon peas, black-eyed peas, and lima beans. Meats included chicken, duck, turkey, beef, and liver and we ate plenty of fish. Our fruit intake included mangoes, bananas, oranges, plums, chenet, and guavas. Except for guava jams and occasional soft drinks, we did not partake of too many simple carbohydrates like candy and other sweets, so the chances for that energy converting into fat were low. Proteins were found in the fish, liver, chicken, duck, and turkey that we consumed.

My mother used a lot of margarine, butter, and shortening for baking and, after learning about trans-fatty acids, I knew I had to make some changes to my cooking style. I felt the need to invest the time and energy to know my body, what my body needed, and what it would take to heal my body or prevent it from getting diseases. I visited an herbalist who helped me further understand the importance of leafy vegetables, root vegetables, fruit, whole grains, legumes, and water in my diet and how the natural foods we eat have an impact on our bodies' function, healing, and, eventually, on how we feel. I was on a mission to make these foods a part of my daily diet, and I succeeded. My herbalist introduced me to other vegetables such as rutabaga, burdock root, turnips, red cabbage, and other whole grains such as quinoa and brown rice, other legumes such as French lentils, red lentils, and different types of nuts and seeds. In addition to what I had learned from my mother in the way of vegetables and legumes, I now had a variety of such foods from which to draw.

In addition to natural foods, I felt that my body needed a booster of green herbal foods, such as spirulina, barley, a good multi-vitamin; and other herbal supplements with anti-oxidant properties such as grape seed extract, flax seed oil, primrose oil, selenium, and fish oil. Research has found that anti-oxidants from food reduce the risk of cancer and heart disease, so although anti-oxidants in pill form will do the same thing, the body reacts better to food than to the pill.[8] This was the main reason that my herbalist suggested that I get nutrition from foods rather than from supplements. Her aim was to help me create a habit of good eating and drinking.

I am not a vegetarian, since I eat baked and broiled fish and chicken at least three times a week. I continue to work out in the gym at least three to five days per week. I have seen major improvement in my health. When illness creeps in, I pray to God concerning my health.

Prayer:

Holy God[9] and God of all comfort,[10]
I confess that I have not always taken care of my body,
Your temple.
I repent for not taking care of my body.
Please forgive me for this sin.
I pray that You would continue
To give me the wisdom to care for
My body in the way that You desire.
In Jesus' name, Amen.

The Lord's reply:

"Do you not know that your body is a temple of the Holy Spirit, who is in you, whom you have received from God? You are not your own; you were bought at a price. Therefore honor God with your body."[11]

Reflection:

Taking exercise can become a chore for me at times, but I make it a point of duty to do so. It is for my good. I remember too, that, so as the things that we do for God will last, so the foods that we put in our bodies will last in either building our bodies or tearing them down.

Your reflection:

What health issues are you facing? List, for example, issues such as high blood pressure and being overweight. What steps are you taking to enable your body to heal itself? If you are on medication, what natural foods can you incorporate into your diet? You may need the help of a nutritionist. Begin to write a daily diet plan for yourself. Exercise and weigh yourself weekly, and record your weight loss. How has your new diet affected your health and your weight?

23

Remembering My Dad

In April, 1985, while teaching at a community college, I felt an urgent need to visit my ailing dad, whom we referred to as "Daddo."

Daddo meant a lot to me. He encouraged me to be my best. However, he was a disciplinarian. We weren't allowed to go out much unless he knew the people with whom we were going. We could not go to parties and have boyfriends until we were of age, twenty to be exact, and when we did, our friends had to visit us at home. We were encouraged to study hard and excel. Daddo did not have the opportunity to finish high school, because his father, his only living parent at the time, had died. However, he had an excellent vocabulary, was widely read, and was knowledgeable in English and Mathematics, so he helped us with our homework. He was critical of us when we did not speak proper English and often lost his temper when we did not do well in school, but would soften up when he received a good school report.

Because Daddo was articulate, I remember him always being involved in politics at the community level and speaking at the corner shop to several people if there was a community event involving speaking.

When my dad was not working, he was involved in the day-to-day issues surrounding our lives, making sure we did our chores and tending to our other needs. When we girls had arguments, he would help us solve our problems by mediating and by giving us opportunities to voice our opinions. We didn't have a voice in other matters, though, for his voice was the final voice, and that was just how things were.

When I was in high school, my dad paid for someone to help my mom do the laundry, starch and iron all the family clothes. He said to my mom one day, "Agnes, Joan is staying up till the wee morning hours to catch up with her studies. We can't have her doing all this work. I know you can't do it either, but we've got to find someone to help with the washing and ironing on Saturdays so she can do her homework."

"John, she can't even get up in the morning," my mom replied. "What yuh say goes."

Because of my father's deep concern for my education, I was freed from excessive housework and was able to use my time more effectively. At one time, my father wanted to buy a family car so I could drive to business school. He took driving lessons, but his second lesson proved to be a disaster. He slammed into a tree and gave up the car idea completely. I never knew why he did not have me try to get my license.

When I was preparing to go to America, my dad made me wool pajamas and two-piece suits. He whispered in my ear, "Don't worry about anything. You are going to make something of yourself and make a way for us." I later sponsored my mother and father as permanent residents in America. They lived in Boston in the early seventies but returned to Trinidad when my father became ill.

My father had a great sense of humor, and when our sons were little, he loved to wrestle with them. Rese and Tony would scream, "Ouch, Grandpa that hurts! Grandpa, you are funny!" My dad would actually bite them while he was wrestling, so he always came out the winner.

So, in April, 1985, I traveled with our daughters, Monique and Jo-An, then eight and two years old, to Trinidad to see Daddo. Monique pushed the carriage while I carried the carry-on luggage. We literally had to run toward the plane in Miami.

I stood to lose my teaching job when I left Boston to visit my father. I was leaving two months before the close of a final semester, and that made me feel insecure. However, the thought of my father passing before I got a chance to see him or hear his last words was frightening. That gave me the zeal to go. As I made my decision, I remembered that when we had earthquakes in Trinidad, my dad, my mother, and us children, would hold each other closely, pray together, and resolve to die together. As a child, I would always say, "If my father should die, I will go with him."

My dad recognized my voice when I arrived and responded with a familiar smile of reassurance that made me feel special. The unsaid words were, "I knew I could count on you to visit me. I'm glad you are here." I, too, was thankful that I was there. I knew that I had done the right thing for him and for me.

At the beginning of January, 1992, I registered for a CPA review course. I was praising God, for I was sure He was preparing me for a job opening through this career path. By April, 1992, I was beset with a desire for a job outside the home. I was praying for the right job, the right money, the right people, and the right environment. I was also undecided about transferring Jo-An to another school where she could get individual help in math, because her present school needed further resources to help her. I continued to pray for protection for my entire family, as if God were not on His throne watching over us.

One Sunday in November, 1992, I was at home brushing up for the CPA examination, scheduled for the following day. As I viewed all the materials strewn across the table, I experienced a strange feeling inside me. I felt deep down that God was taking me in another direction and that probably I should no longer pursue the CPA career path. At mid-morning, I received a telephone call from Trinidad stating that my father had died. My prayer was, "Lord, what shall I do?" I wondered if I would get my refund, but, most importantly, I was wondering about taking the test again and realizing that I would have to wait a whole year to do so. I knew I had to be decisive. I was. I assisted in the planning of and attended my father's funeral.

Some of my associates advised me to live my own life since my dad was already dead. "Let the dead bury their own dead," one friend remarked. However, I listened to my heart and felt that I had made the right decision. I attended to all aspects of the funeral.

My extended family members, emotional as they were, did not handle my father's death very well. Family disputes emerged at every level during and after the funeral process, but I lived through them. I was attending the funeral to see my dad for the last time. He was worth my time!

Prayer:

The heavens declare the glory of God,
And the firmament shows his handiwork.[1]
Lord, I confess the enormous grief and sadness
That I feel over the loss of my dad.
He was dear to me,
Patient with me,
And loved me for the person I am.
He encouraged me to be my best.
Thank You for giving him longevity of life.[2]
Lord, I pray that You would help me to
Overcome my grief and
Pick up the pieces of my life again.
In Jesus' name, Amen.

The Lord's reply:

"A father of the fatherless and
a judge for the widows,
Is God in His holy habitation."[3]

Reflection:

God's love surpasses all the love that I could have received from my dad.

Your reflection:

Maybe, you have had a good relationship with your earthly father. Maybe, you have lost a father or have never received a father's love. Reflect on how God has been a Father to you and how He has helped you and continues to be there for you. Confess your feeling of rejection to God; ask for His forgiveness, and accept His love for you.

24

Struggling to Know God's Will

Returning to my immediate family was a relief after Daddo's funeral. I was thankful for how God had guided me through the entire process. I continued to give God thanks for everything: for keeping me under the umbrella of His wings, for loving me, for bringing me out of the miry clay, and setting my feet on solid ground. I began to thank Him for my circumstances, recognizing that when I was out of control, He was in control of my life; thanking Him that He was making a way out for me, that He was lighting my lamp, and thanking Him for being patient with me during my entire life. I prayed that God would set me apart to minister the gifts of comfort and healing to many.

During my pain and struggle, God continued to fill my heart with joy. I had joy just seeing our children happy. In June, 1993, Monique was off to her junior prom dressed in a bottle green, knee-length dress. She and her friends looked gorgeous in their prom dresses.

By July, 1993, however, I was struggling to know God's will for my life. I continued to ask God to teach me to wait on Him, to wash me thoroughly with hyssop, to make my heart as white as snow, to remind me that I am His and that no one can snatch me out of His hands. In my prayer, I told God how much I loved Him and that I was leaving all to follow Him. I discerned that God had a purpose for me, and I began to ask Him to reveal it to me, to guide and give me strength for the battle ahead. I had no idea that battles were indeed raging and that God was giving me strength to go through impending storms.

Prayer:

Oh, how I love Jesus!
Oh, how I love Jesus!
Because He first loved me.[1]
Lord, You are a great God;
You are worthy of all praise and honor.[2]
Lord, I confess my reluctance to submit to Your will.
I repent of this sin and pray that
You would forgive me Lord, for my disobedience.
Lord, God, thank You for being my Father.[3]
Thank You for loving me.[4]
Thank You for keeping me.[5]
Thank You for making a way for me,
When there was no way.[6]
Thank You for being patient[7] with me
In the midst of my difficulties and my loss.
Teach me to wait on You, God,

Until You reveal Your purpose for me.
I pray this in Jesus' name, Amen.

The Lord's reply:

"But those who hope in the LORD
will renew their strength.
They will soar on wings like eagles;
they will run and not grow weary;
they will walk and not be faint."[8]

Reflection:

God yearns for a relationship with us. He wants us to talk to Him and get to know Him intimately.

Your reflection:

Reflect on areas in your life where you have not submitted to God's will. Confess this lack of submission to God, and ask Him for patience to wait on Him.

25

Facing Challenges

In 1995, Carl and I faced our first major challenge. Our son Rese was finishing his paperwork for college. The very day that he was to sign his dormitory card, he was called to the police station, detained for questioning, and arrested on armed robbery charges. We felt that our dream for him to have a college career was over. Prior to his conviction, our son had been in and out of court several times and had been put on probation. He had violated probation as a result of his arrest in 1995, and therefore, was ordered to serve time for his new, as well as for his previous convictions.

Rese could not justify choosing this lifestyle, especially knowing the type of family from which he came. Carl and I had worked hard and brought up our children right. Rese explained to me in January of 2008 what had happened:

"My cousin and I went to a movie, and we got robbed on the train and lost jewelry and money. That experience changed my way of thinking—no longer would I be a prey but a predator, and so I began to

adapt to my environment, involving myself in criminal activities."

He also explained why he continued this lifestyle after he was freed on previous charges:

"I was always getting bailed out, so I thought I was invincible. The judge saw that I came from a good family, and so I would always get breaks."

Carl and I never had to face a situation like that. We were in utter dismay, walking around without knowing where to turn and whom to call. We had no one to talk to who would understand our ongoing pain, so we kept it to ourselves. I couldn't fathom the depth of Carl's pain, because he didn't talk too much about it. He continued to enjoy his routines after work and on weekends: swimming, making and drinking his smoothies, eating lots of fruit and nuts, listening to music, doing laundry, reading, and resting.

I was still operating a home-based business and was facing my son's issues and my mother's illness simultaneously. My youngest sister had gone to Trinidad to care for my mother and returned to Boston with her, so that my mother could receive treatment. It was the very month our son was arrested, convicted, and made to serve a three to five year sentence for violating probation for his prior cases. My mother had a terminal illness which lasted until her death in July of 1995. My son's sentencing for his current conviction did not come until a year and a half later. What a disaster that was for me! I was faced with two sources of problems, and that fact left my husband Carl and me with even more to handle.

Rese's sentencing was the greatest challenge I had ever faced. Carl had gone to court repeatedly with our son before and didn't feel that he could face the sentencing. I decided to go. I knew no one else would—not even relatives. No one.

I felt lonely and helpless, experiencing self-pity in the courtroom, as I had to stand several times to answer the judge's questions. She was kind, proud of us parents, and saddened by what she had to pronounce—5 to 7 years. I sat there embracing what I had left of my emotions. There was no joy, no peace, only emptiness and a sense of failure as I witnessed our son being taken away in shackles. I composed myself, tried to relax, and didn't cry, because I thought to myself, "What good would that do?" I realized that my composure was because I was not alone, for God was sitting right beside me, carrying me through the entire process of that difficult day.

Recently, Rese explained how he, too, had felt on that day:

"My heart dropped. I felt like my whole world came to an end. Life was over—a feeling of being dead but yet alive. There was a feeling of hopelessness, no light at the end of the tunnel. Darkness. I didn't feel like killing myself, because I was too strong for that; but at the same time, it was a feeling of not wanting to go on. The question that was plaguing me was, 'Why was this happening to me?' "

Carl and I had to continue with our lives, yet, without giving up on our son. I sometimes accompanied my husband Carl on his monthly visits to the prison. We were eager to visit our son, talk to him, and give him encouragement.

I disliked the process we had to go through on our visits. We had to take off our shoes and were searched. I couldn't wear jewelry or have pins in my hair. I felt that we were robbed of our individualities and privacy, but we visited because Rese was our son—God's child. God had a plan for his life.

Together, Carl and I experienced pain, loneliness, anguish, brokenness, self-pity, guilt, blame, and shame. I blamed Carl for being lenient with our son. I blamed myself for not following through with firm parental actions that might have kept our son from trouble. Whatever we did, we could not remove the pain and, worse yet, the shame that engulfed our lives. There were unanswered questions plaguing our minds: What had gone wrong? Why did it happen? Who was to blame for the mishap? We had lived a pretty good life, had good jobs, raised our children well, provided them with a good education and extracurricular activities, including various sports, music, and swimming classes. Where had we gone wrong?

I had been operating in a self-contained bubble inside a box, where my world was secure, safe, and unshakable. Now, my world was shaken. We felt the torment of self-inflicted failure—failure that was not real, but shallow and unjustified. Carl and I tried to explain the situations that we faced by turning to God in order to understand God's plans for our lives and those of our sons and daughters.

"Have you ever thought, Carl, that God is using this situation to bring us closer to Him?" I asked one day.

"God has never failed me yet," Carl said. "When I was in school, I wrote notes to God. I still have those notes up to this day. He has never failed me. He knows best."

"God is definitely protecting Rese," I replied. "Deep down, Carl, I sense that God has a ministry in the future for Rese. We can't lose heart. God is preparing him for a great work. He is going to be a great man of God. Remember when Rese was four years old, that he was always lying on our bed listening to me read the Bible to him. I know God is faithful.

He will bring it to pass."

Days, months, and years flew by. Rese was absent for major family events. We continued to receive numerous letters from him, telling us how much he loved us and that we had to hold on—that we are family, and that he would be home soon. He explained this in the following excerpts of his letter of April, 1997:

Dear Moms,

How are you doing? I'm doing alright, so I hope you are doing alright. I'm glad to see that your faith is building more and more. It is a big test, and I know you will pass. Mammy, I hope you know that you are an excellent mother, and I hope Carl knows as well that he is an excellent father. I know sometimes you might think about me now and then, and probably all sorts of thoughts might be going through your head, but you have to remember what happened to me is my fault, not anybody else's. I was a very selfish man, and I know everything happens for a reason. Life is not over, and the future is near as long as the clock is still ticking. Whenever any of us goes through trials, it makes us stronger as a person. It builds our faith even more.

All I worry about is my immediate family; if you are alright, I am alright. Mammy, I love you and please continue to keep strong, because only the strong survives. I will be home soon.

P.S. Tell the family I love them and to keep the faith. You are always with me no matter where I am.

Love,

Your son

Rese

He explained his experiences in prison, how he was able to deal with life in prison, and the vision that God gave him the fifth year in prison:

"Life in prison was hectic. You had to have a powerful mind. The system would drain you mentally— they told you when to eat, when to sleep, and when to go to the bathroom. If you did not have hope, it was easy for you to fall prey to that system again and again, by being in and out of prison your whole life and not realizing it.

I came from a very good family so basically, I knew what it was like to be good. I had a vision the fourth or fifth year I was in prison. I was looking out the window, into the sky, and God showed me my entire life all in one moment and told me the way I was living was not the way to live. I realized that I had to make a complete turnaround. At that moment, I had a vision and a plan—a vision to see myself successfully operating a barber salon, and so I named it right there and then."

The difficulty for Rese came in early 2001, when he was released. He had a great deal of relearning to do and many things with which to catch up, but he also had a plan. He was very sensitive, so we were careful how we spoke and what we said around him. He also observed that his sister and brother were doing well, and that gave him the incentive to do likewise. This is how he explained his transition from prison to praise and the motivation he received to do it:

"My immediate family was acting like I was a brand new baby in the world. Because I was taken away from society so long, I forgot what it felt like to be free and to adapt to society—doing easy things like getting an ID, using a cell phone, using a CD player, answering a phone, taking a shower without slippers, and sleeping before 9:30 p.m. I had difficulty

recognizing extended family members."

"But, difficult as things were, I was determined to succeed. I took my old hustling manner of life and applied it in positive ways. I was always good socially, and had my way with people. I knew I had to live a totally opposite life now—not being seen—low keyed—and not having friends either, because all my friends were bad. I stayed to myself or with positive people like my immediate family. I was forced to do well because of the examples before me. I knew I had to make sacrifices by following the plan that God had given me—a plan to live differently, one that would help me achieve my goals. I listened to God continually, and He helped me in the process. Nothing was easy. The more difficult the goal, the harder I worked to achieve it. If it was easy, it wasn't meant for me to have it, because I didn't have to sacrifice to achieve it. I was constantly faced with trials and tribulations to get where I wanted to go. It was going through pain to reach glory."

Rese started working in a fast food store, then in a barber salon. About a year later, he started his own barber salon, purchased a car with his brother co-signing for him, and now owns his own home.

As I reviewed the issues of the past, thoughts went through my head. I realized I still did not have answers to life's challenges. I could only lay them down at the feet of Jesus, so I prayed.

Prayer:

Lord, God, I come before You, my God, glorious God![1]

I praise You and magnify Your Name,

Which is above every name in heaven, and in earth.[2]

I confess my feelings of guilt, blame, and shame.
I repent of my sins of guilt, blame, and shame.
Please forgive me Lord, for these sins.
Thank You, Father, that because of Jesus' death,
My sins were nailed to the Cross.[3]
I pray that You would make a way for Carl and me
To experience peace and joy again.
Help us to know that our strength comes from You.[4]
In Jesus' name, Amen.

The Lord's reply:

"Peace I leave with you; my peace I give you. I do not give to you as the world gives.
Do not let your hearts be troubled and do not be afraid.[5]
For the joy of the Lord is your strength."[6]

Reflection:

I look at Rese's life now as a testimony to God's faithfulness. Christ was molding and shaping him according to His perfect plan into the person that God had called him to be. God has given him divine favor.

Your reflection:

Hold the hands of your son or your daughter; look him or her straight in the face, and tell him or her how much God loves him or her and how much you love him or her. Reflect on how God has forgiven you; forgive your son or daughter for the trouble he or she has caused you, and reassure him or her that God has a plan and a purpose for his or her life.

26

Surrendering All to Christ

In June, 2001, I was at West Yarmouth on my yearly retreat to rest and reassess my life. I checked into a hotel at 3 p.m. that afternoon, rested a bit, and had dinner about 7 p.m. The fish dinner was not exceptional. I have had better. The restaurant was a bit noisy and crowded, too. Not having my car limited me to nearby restaurants; however, I enjoyed walking and viewing scenic Cape Cod. I bought juice and a piece of fruit for my evening snack and proceeded to my hotel room. That night, I began reviewing my journals from 1983 onward.

I perused my journals quickly. The first portion of my journals revealed that I was frustrated at times, wanting my freedom and complete control of my life, and when I did not get what I wanted, it seemed that I resorted to being rebellious toward God, my Father, despite all that He continued to do for me. I was praying for God to give me things and change my circumstances but never asking God for His will to be done. I was angry and frustrated, blaming my husband when problems arose instead of praying to God about the situation and leaving it in His hands. I devoted many years to inner struggles rather than focusing on God's purpose for my life.

I continued to peruse these pages the next morning on a lawn chair at the makeshift beach at the rear of the hotel. I could see the bay ahead. The skies were blue, the air fresh, and the sun shining. "Surely this is the way to enjoy life, even temporarily," I thought.

Clearly, the Holy Spirit was revealing to me who I was. I recognized my sins of disobedience, pride, control, rebellion, un-forgiveness, insecurity, fear, and procrastination; asked God's forgiveness, and promised to utterly depend on Him. I confirmed God's love for me, noting that He wanted the best for me, His best. I asked God to guide and direct me and to provide me with what I needed rather than what I wanted. I asked that my life be lived for His glory only. At that retreat, the Lord was instructing me to surrender all to Him.

Prayer:

Lord, I praise and adore You, Mighty God![1]
I confess that I have not surrendered every
Area of my life to You.
I now repent and ask Your forgiveness
For my stubbornness.
I pray now, and surrender my life,
All that I am and all that I could ever be,
To Your care.
Make me, mold me, and fashion me, Lord,

According to Your perfect plan and will
For my life.
In Jesus' name, Amen.

The Lord's reply:

"If my people, who are called by my name, will humble themselves and pray and seek my face and turn from their wicked ways, then will I hear from heaven and, will forgive their sin and will heal their land."[2]

Reflection:

Submitting to God includes worshiping, praising, confessing, praying, seeking, listening, and waiting on Him.

Your reflection:

Reflect on a particular time in your life when you rebelled and did not surrender to God's will. Describe how you were rebellious toward God and how your rebellion prevented you from surrendering to God's will. How were you able to get back on track?

27

Remembering My Mother

My mother Agnes was slightly heavy, with a rounded face and olive skin. We called her "Mammy." Mammy wore dresses and skirts even at home, and she wore her grey hair in single braids. When she went out, she would pull her hair back into a bun to look elegant. She wore glasses. My mother never worked outside the home, except when she was a seamstress, designing bridal and other clothing for people in the community, but that was long before she had us kids. She also designed all of our clothes, making us beautiful dresses for church, for Easter or for special occasions.

My mother, although less learned than my father, spoke to teachers on our behalf. She had the smile, the drive, and the energy to speak to people in high places. She always found the words to say. She got us into good schools and part-time jobs when school was out. In our growing up years, we did not have a whole lot, yet, we were one of the best-dressed families in the neighborhood, and we ate the most delicious meals. What I remember most was that life had meaning and that my parents instilled in us the need to work hard if we were to reach our potential and achieve our goals.

One of the anxieties that I had for a long time was pleasing my mother, who wanted me to become a certified public accountant. That thought lived with me throughout my marriage. Not feeling complete, I tried financial planning, ordered the books to study, made deposits on the course, and then changed my mind. I knew that a business degree was all that I wanted to pursue in college. Interestingly, when I attended college, I noticed that I always took religious courses as electives. Later, I found out why.

My mother and I spoke briefly on the telephone in early December, 1994. She wanted me to visit her in Trinidad for the Christmas season. A December visit meant no Christmas for the rest of my family, since I did all of the cooking, baking, and shopping. Also, we just did not have the finances to take our entire family to Trinidad. As a result, I postponed the visit to January, 1995. I had no idea that my mother was dying and wanted me to spend time with her.

During our January visit, Monique, Jo-An, and I stayed at my mother's house, which was located in a small, working class village, which gave us access to local taxis, buses, churches, mom and pop stores, downtown Port-of-Spain, and surrounding areas. The house had been renovated into a two-story brick house and did not have the cozy feeling of our old wooden, two-bedroom home, with which we were accustomed. The house sat on a hill overlooking the street, which gave it beauty and uniqueness. Wild tropical plants covered the front and side landscape, and mango trees compassed the rear yard. It was easy to secure a mango from the hanging branches of the mango trees laden with mangoes. Also in the rear of the yard, my mother kept her washing tub and ribbed scrubbing board, used for washing clothes by hand. After hand-washing the clothes, my mother would lay them flat on rectangular, meshed tables we called "bleaches" for the sun and rain to further clean them. After a day or so, she would rewash them and rinse them being careful to use starch on white shirts and a blue liquid we called "blue" to give them a whiter appearance. After rinsing and starching, she would put the clothes on a clothesline to dry.

Mammy was very committed to caring for us, especially when we were ill. As a child, I suffered with asthma, and I believe that my healing was a result of my mother's faith in the healing power of God and of her diligent care of me. She would wake up during the night and put hot towels on my chest to ease the pain and to help me breathe easier. She would also give me cod liver oil and vitamins daily to build my immune system.

She was a hard-working woman, working in the house, cooking, cleaning, washing, and ironing. For breakfast, Mammy made us fried and roast bakes, cornmeal cereal, sago, and other types of porridges. She also prepared all types of herbal teas from the leaves that she secured from her garden.

There was always flour on Mammy's apron, on the table, or on the concrete counter near the stove. To make fried bakes, she rolled the dough in small ball-like shapes and flattened them on the palm of her hand, then cooked them in olive oil in a pan on the stove. The bakes were lightly brown and crispy. To make a roasted bake from the same dough, she took a larger portion of the dough and rolled it into a large circle and baked it in the oven until it was lightly brown and moist. Mammy prepared buljol or accra which complemented the bakes.

Mammy made the most scrumptious meals, deserts, and juices. She cooked soups with cornmeal dumplings in them. Every meal came with a side order of vegetables and legumes. On Sundays, Mammy cooked macaroni pie (baked macaroni) or potato salad with our meals. During the week, she cooked curried dishes, pelau, and an array of root vegetables including dasheen and edoes. On the days when Mammy fried or stewed king fish, red fish, and shark, she included a side dish of coo-coo.

She made deserts such as home-made ice-cream, sugar cakes (a brown, crunchy desert with coconut and spices), and black cake and sweetbread at holiday time. She made us juices such as mauby (from mauby bark), ginger beer (from grated ginger), sorrel, and juices from various fruits.

Mammy cooked to please her husband and us her children. When my father came home, he knew he could count on Mammy to have a hot meal waiting. Because Mammy was engrossed in her daily chores of cooking, cleaning, and laundering, she never left the house except when she went to the central market to buy food for our family or to attend church services. I remember accompanying my mother to the marketplace every Saturday when I was a young girl. She would spend a long time in the marketplace, not only shopping, but also stopping periodically to talk to everyone she met. I would stand there for fifteen or twenty minutes waiting for my mother to finish her conversation with each person. I couldn't continue with shopping, because only my mother had the ability to stretch the little money she had and buy all that she needed, and besides, she always hid a roll of money inside her blouse to prevent it from being lost or misplaced.

She would sometimes introduce me to several women as my second and third cousins, people whom I had never met and whose names I never remembered. She would say, for example, "This is yuh cousin Hilda, yuh know." I would smile and bend forward to hug the person. Our custom was to show love and respect to an elder. Doing anything else was unheard of. I hated when a relative kissed me and left wet marks on my cheeks.

My mother loved to fix our lunches for school. She would even pack an extra lunch in case there was a student who could not afford a lunch. Carrying two sets of lunches was really burdensome, particularly considering that my mother used old metal containers and packed hot lunches: rice in one container and peas and meat in another, making four containers altogether.

She was known to be a Good Samaritan. On rainy days, my mother would reach out to children walking home from school who were soaking wet from the rain. She would offer a bowl of soup and a change of clothing to each student. She never visited a neighbor unless that person was sick. Mammy would repeatedly call out to her neighbors and ask how they were doing, and they would ask how she was doing as well. This was a normal way of life in our village. If she was hanging clothes on the line at the rear of the house, she would call out to her neighbors: "Good morning Ms. Jackman. How yuh're keepin?"

And Ms. Jackman would reply, "I'm not so good, yuh know. The artritis is bodering me again."

My mother would prescribe medication for Ms. Jackman: "Yuh must use some bengai and rob duh legs, mann."

If anyone was in need of anything, that person could go to my mother. She often assisted a mother across the street by shampooing and combing her children's hair. My mother was basically a good person.

Mammy was the matriarch of the family, one whom everyone looked to for emotional support. It was a strategy that made her seem strong and secure. As long as she was the focus of receiving information and offering advice, all was well.

However, there was another side to my mother. She was a woman who kept grudges. In Trinidad, she never forgave a woman who wanted to reconcile their differences. The woman eventually died, and my mother never felt remorseful. Mammy got herself in family conflicts because she could not keep secrets. She was not one to sit down and discuss life issues with us or tell us how much she loved us, although she showed love by the way she cared for us. I think she had difficulty in that area and just could not handle herself emotionally. Mammy was never satisfied with the choices I made wanting the first and last say in my life. That angered me for a long time. I knew that once I came to America, attended college and got married, that she could no longer dominate my life and that I was finally free.

My mother always wanted to care for one of my children. I never believed in having someone else raise our children, but it was common to have grandparents in Trinidad raising their first grandchild. Although Rese was our second child, she would say to me, "Give me Rese, nuh?" or she would say to him, "Come and live with yuh Gramma, boy, all duh girls will go crazy over yuh." My mother always tried to encourage me to return to Trinidad. She was forever trying to convince me by saying, "Girl, you won't go back to live in Trinidad? With your degrees, yuh'll get a big job, yuh know." I just did not like her manipulation, but I never told her about it. I respected my mother a great deal and would never hurt her feelings.

When our son Tony was born, she followed tradition and invited me to stay a week in her apartment to assist me. By the third or fourth day, I left my mother's home, disgusted over her manipulation and domineering attitude. However, I was thankful for her continued help with Tony while Carl and I worked full-time.

When my mother turned eighty, my sisters, brother, our spouses, and I had a small party for her at the Top of the Hub in Boston. My mother received roses and other gifts. She enjoyed the great seafood dinner. She was overjoyed when the pianist played a happy birthday song to her while the waitress brought her a birthday cake.

Although I had issues with my mother, I always found the time to take her to doctor's appointments or to church services while she lived in America. I learned to tolerate my mother and to love her for who she was.

Prayer:

Worthy is the Lamb, Who was slain, to receive power
And wealth and wisdom and strength and honor and glory
And praise.[1]
Lord, I confess at times,
That I did not show love to my mother.
I repent of my failure to love her, Lord,
And pray that You would forgive me
For sinning against You.
I pray for courage, strength, endurance, and
Patience in order to understand,
And be at peace with my mother.
In Jesus' name, Amen.

The Lord's reply:

"Honor your father and mother, as the LORD your God has commanded

you, so that you
may live long and that it may go well with you in the land the LORD
your God is giving you."[2]

Reflection:

I reflect on the times that I kept my feelings to myself, only to feel angry and resentful. Eventually, I had to release my anger. Today, I am relieved that I utilized control and was respectful to my parents.

Your reflection:

Reflect on a moment when you just blew it or were aggravated with your mom, stepmom, aunt, cousin, or grandmother, whether that person is alive or deceased. How else could you have handled the situation? Explain what you learned from handling the situation correctly or incorrectly? Release that issue or those issues to God and begin to walk the road of reconciliation with that important person by forgiving her or yourself.

28

Dealing with My Mother's Illness and Her Passing

On our visit to Trinidad in January, 1995, my mother looked very thin and frail. She had no zeal to do the usual: attend church services, go to the market, cook, or eat. She employed a young male assistant who did most of her cooking and cleaning and made all the decisions for her. That she no longer made decisions put a strain on our relationship during our visit with her.

At one point, she brought up issues of the past that made my daughters and I feel uncomfortable, so we decided to go on picnics and visit other relatives and friends. We felt the tension as we left and returned from our daily trips. I wanted to prove to her that I was not going to fall prey to her behavior, and my actions said it all.

In April, 1995, my youngest sister traveled to Trinidad because my mother had taken a turn for the worse. Her exact condition was not quite clear, but the decision to bring her to Boston for treatment was made, then all became clear. She had known she was very ill and had wanted me to spend Christmas with her. When I had visited in January, I had been focused on my children and myself. I wanted to have a good time, not realizing that my mother was ill. Once I discovered the extent of her illness, I felt guilty for my failure to spend time with her in a meaningful way.

In May, 1995, she was admitted to a local hospital in Boston and was diagnosed with cancer and had just a few months to live. We were going to lose our mother. I was working at home, so at times I joined my youngest sister and her husband, who made daily visits to the hospital to be at my mother's bedside. I knew that my mother was in constant pain, and that could explain her lack of expression. Her watery eyes seemed to stare into oblivion, not focusing on the people around her but knowing they were there. She ate when I fed her, and I felt satisfied about that. She never acknowledged the prayers that I said on her behalf. She showed signs of depression and disappointment when her attending physician informed her of the seriousness of her illness and that she had only a short time to live. To this day, I am not sure whether my mother had prepared herself to meet her Maker. But of course, who am I to judge her?

In June, 1995, my youngest sister asked that my mother be moved to her home. There, I painfully watched my mother deteriorate as her time approached. My other sisters and I took turns caring for her, but the bulk of the responsibility remained on my sister and her husband, who were constantly at my mother's bedside, bathing her, changing her, feeding her, and providing for her every need.

My mother's passing was sudden and frightening for all of us, especially for my youngest sister. She called me in the middle of the night when my mother died in July, 1995.

"Joan, Mammy just died. I have never experienced this, so I'm a little frightened. However, Mammy looks the prettiest she has ever been."

She did look peaceful when she died. Death had never come so close to our doors (except for when our father had passed in November of 1992), so we were both nervous, teeth chattering, shivering, and speechless. After calling a funeral home to fetch the body, my sister and I had a good night's sleep and began the funeral arrangements the following day; the burial was to take place in Trinidad during the month of August.

Although we made many of the arrangements in Boston, we were still running around making last-minute plans in Trinidad. The funeral service was held at a Roman Catholic cathedral among some of my mother's closest friends and only a fraction of her relatives. The service was short and did not have the kind of family involvement that one gets here in the United States.

After burial, friends and family members gathered nightly to pray, support, and comfort each other. Families shared by bringing food and drink. I felt strange taking a leadership role, a role that my mother previously had: cooking, making the necessary preparations, and welcoming guests as they came by. Having left Trinidad many years ago, I had to be re-introduced to a few relatives.

I faced constant conflicts with extended family members both during and after the funeral arrangements. I felt uncomfortable and wished I was at home. However, God strengthened me during the process.

Prayer:

My Lord and my God,

My strength and my shield,[1]
Lord, thank You that You are
As near to me as my breath.[2]
You promise never to leave or
Forsake me.[3]
Thank You for Your protection.[4]
I pray for strength
During this difficult time.
In Jesus' name, Amen.

The Lord's reply:

"My grace is sufficient
for you, for my power is made perfect in weakness."[5]

Reflection:

Families experience emotional times when a loved one dies. Some families, including my extended family, do not handle funerals well. At times, we have to take the good with the bad, write off the bad debts in our lives, forgive, and move on.

Your reflection:

Maybe you experienced a family feud under circumstances other than a funeral. Reflect on what happened. Did your feelings get hurt, or did you hurt someone's feelings? If so, describe how you were able to forgive or reconcile differences between you and that family member. If you were not able to reconcile with your family member, pray, and ask God to show you how to begin the process of reconciliation.

29

Taking a New Job/New Challenges

In January, 1996, my husband Carl informed me that a government agency had openings for full-time auditors and that I stood a good chance of obtaining one of the positions advertised in the local paper. I prepared a functional resume describing my experiences. I wanted the resume to be printed on off-white paper stock matching the envelope, but after missing the application deadline, I decided to take the chance and mail it as it was. What did I have to lose? I sought career counseling to help me with the interviewing process. Amazingly, I received a call for both an initial and follow-up interview, and was offered a position as a full-time auditor.

My career was off to a good start when God provided for me in January, 1996. I was extremely happy but also a bit anxious. I received my initial six-month training under an experienced auditor before being on my own. With laptop in hand and professionally dressed, I went from company to company and performed audits. I liked the fact that I was out of the office and managed my own caseload. I was really getting a handle on my job and beginning to like it a lot when my life began to turn again for the worse.

Jo-An, our youngest, twelve and a half years old at the time, was experiencing a mental breakdown and could not focus in school. Jo-An was quiet and preferred to read at recess rather than make friends. However, she always managed to have at least one or two friends. She was well read and had a wide vocabulary; she loved to go to the library and borrow books, read for long hours in her room, write poems and short stories. She was very good with computers at a young age. She designed our invitations for our anniversary celebration in February, 1996. She enjoyed ballet dancing and celebrating her annual birthday party with family and friends.

In June, 1996, Jo-An's progress at school came to a halt. I met with Jo-An's teacher, who was at a loss to know how to get her focused again. She suggested a major task at school to encourage her involvement, so Jo-An's task was to ensure that everyone understood his or her part for a class play. Jo-An had informed me that she had misplaced the instructions. In April of 1996, I noticed the anxiety in her voice. I decided that we should call each student to explain his or her part. As we sat and called each student, I knew in my heart that Jo-An was experiencing something unusual. She was unable to finish her examinations by the end of the school year. Although she returned to school that September, it was obvious that by December, we were going to face the challenge of finding alternative placement for her. Our journey with Jo-An was non-stop from that point on.

Our beautiful Jo-An needed a different type of care, care that was foreign to us. The lives of our entire family began to change. We did everything in our power to work at changing the situation, to make it right so we could make our lives more comfortable, but the situation never got better. In fact, it got worse. Tensions brewed in our home as the situation got worse, and I was pressed from every side to give up on Jo-An and to live my own life. But even in the midst of the pain, the stress, and the insecurity of life, God gave me strength for the journey ahead.

The months flew by, and my work was the only thing that kept me busy and occupied enough to pass the time and mask the pain; although, every break I got, I was consumed with making appointments, talking to doctors, social workers, and school staff. I went home every day thinking and talking about the situations that confronted us. Jo-An was experiencing emotional upheaval. We did not have a clue how to help her. We relied on school personnel to guide us accordingly. This was new. Different. Scary.

Prayer:

I come to you, Mighty God,[1]
Thanking You, Lord God, for being
My present help in the time of trouble.[2]
Lord, I confess the pain, the stress,
And insecurity that I feel as I deal with my
Daughter's condition and her future,
Worrying how she would make it
If I were not around to care for her.
I repent of these sins, and, Lord,
I pray that You would forgive me
For carrying these burdens.
I pray for a new measure of faith in You,
That would allow me to face my current situation

With confidence.
In Jesus' name, Amen.

The Lord's reply:

"If you have faith as small as a mustard seed, you can say to this mountain, 'Move from here to there' and it will move. Nothing will be impossible for you."[3]

"And without faith it is impossible to please God, because anyone who comes to him must believe that he exists and that he rewards those who earnestly seek him."[4]

Reflection:

That experience was overwhelming; I dealt with my situation by constantly praying and seeking God daily. When I entrusted Jo-An to God's care, dealing with her situation became much easier.

Your reflection:

Have you recently been faced with a situation that has given you stress, pain, and grief? How are you handling your situation? Try turning the entire situation over to God. Pray for guidance, and, reflect on how your situation has changed, since you have turned it over to God. Write your reflections here.

30

Learning through Trials

Jo-An needed special care; we engaged a local psychiatric hospital which had started an adolescent day program. We enrolled Jo-An in their day program from December 1996 to January 1997 before placing her in a special needs school in February of 1997. Carl and I alternated in getting her at the end of the day. Initially, all seemed to be going well. When she returned to the hospital between June and July 1997 for psychiatric treatment, things began to change.

When Carl and I requested a team meeting, we found out that doctors had injected Jo-An, at age thirteen, with adult doses of Haldol medication, which we believe had debilitating effects on her brain, impairing her ability to communicate, write, or read. When I would visit her in the hospital where this took place, she drooled profusely, could not eat, and was given tomato soup for dinner. Instead of getting better, Jo-An was progressively getting worse. We had meetings with the treatment team, who suggested that Jo-An be part of a study that the senior psychiatrist was conducting in Washington to find the drug that would benefit her.

When we refused, the psychiatrist insisted on sending her to a state mental institution, telling us that she would never read or write, except color with crayons, at best. We wanted to take our daughter home by her birthday in September; when we realized that was not going to happen we secured a transfer to another hospital to obtain a second opinion.

The psychiatrist at the second hospital took her off her current medications to clean her system and give her body time to adjust to new medications. However, after a month, he decided that Jo-An should be sent to a state mental institution, and told us that if we did not comply with his recommendation, he would take us to court. He had given us information about a day treatment center, so on the eve of Jo-An's discharge, Carl and I urgently and quickly applied to this center, and Jo-An was accepted. The psychiatrist understood, I believe, our plight as parents, and decided not to take us to court.

In July, 2000, when it seemed that our daughter's life was going downhill, I took a leave of absence from my new job after being there for four and a half years. My one-year leave turned into two and a half years. I was on a mission to help Jo-An, a mission that my family felt didn't make practical sense. Our lives were in chaos. I felt alone. As my trials intensified, I had no other recourse but to pray, seek God's wisdom, wait on Him, and obey His voice. In August of 2000, I took our daughter off all the medications she was taking. The process was very slow, and at times, I doubted whether I was doing the right thing, but as the months turned into years, Jo-An's health became stable. I replaced the medication with herbal therapy, which I had researched, and which included grape-seed extract, flax seed, liquid B-complex vitamins, a liquid multi-vitamin, selenium, and ginkgo biloba. I mixed these into a smoothie with strawberries, seeds, walnuts, and lecithin. This she took daily. I made it a point to give Jo-An a walk three times per week for fifteen minutes, at a small park, which was not too busy and not too far from our home. It was not easy giving her walks. If I didn't hold her hand and walk briskly, she would stop and pick up twigs and leaves, and our walking times would have been endless. I persevered.

Since my life was hectic, I would wake up in the early morning hours and pray to God in my home office. I would cry and cry and desperately ask God to heal our daughter, but nothing extraordinary resulted from my prayers. I was praying and crying out to God continuously. I was getting impatient with the situation before me and was wondering whether I would get any release. Would I get help? I was asking, "God, where are you in all of this?" I was in the greatest fire I had ever experienced, but I knew that God had promised to rescue me. I was asking, "How long, Lord? How long?"

We tried hospitalizations, a day treatment center, special schools, therapists, medication, but nothing worked. In August of 2000, on the advice of family and friends, I took Jo-An to a healing service at Worcester Centrum, where a leading Evangelist was preaching. Jo-An got to the Centrum and sat quietly, but when she wanted to go to the restroom, I left my belongings with someone and proceeded to walk out of the aisle. In the space of one minute, Jo-An had disappeared, and I could not find her anywhere. I thought, "What will Carl think of me if I return home without Jo-An?" I began to pray, "God, You are my present help in the time of trouble (Ps.46:1). Lord, please show me where Jo-An is?" I walked down the street, and there she was. I recognized her by the bright pink shirt she was wearing and by her tall, slender figure. I ran as fast as I could until I caught up with her. I held her hand, and together, we walked back to the Centrum and onto the stage. Jo-An was not healed! I wanted to try everything, but I had taken a big step driving Jo-An to the Centrum and staying overnight in a hotel with her. I was desperate.

During July, 2002, Carl, Monique, and Rese went to Trinidad for a two-week vacation, so I did not have support; it was not easy, but I was bent on relying on God. I realized that I wasn't being good to myself, so I made a decision to make the local YMCA my place of refuge for my workouts and relaxation. Our son Tony was in town, so he came over occasionally to spend time with Jo-An.

In late October, 2002, the School Department provided weekly tutoring sessions for Jo-An at home while they began the long road of finding a school placement for her. On October 21, 2002, I was asking God, how was I going to get Jo-An to her first interview at Weymouth, Massachusetts? I knew that was going to be challenging. I woke up at 6:30 a.m. that morning, got myself showered and dressed, ironed Jo-An's clothes, and made breakfast for us both. I went to Jo-An's room, gently moved the covers from her face, and informed her about the appointment. Her response was, "Leave me alone," suggesting that she was not interested in anything I said and that she had no intention of going anywhere.

I declared, "I am giving you five minutes to get off this bed, and I will return."

I was pacing the floor back and forth, seeking God's direction. I felt trapped. I felt frustrated. I wanted a new beginning, and that meant wanting change. I returned to Jo-An's room and again removed the covers from her face. I told her firmly, "Jo-An, you are going with me to your appointment. I want you to know that God loved you before the foundation of the world. You have hope, and you have the power to walk away from the things that make you sad. In the name of Jesus, I command you to take a shower." Lo and behold, Jo-An got up and walked straight to the bathroom. I was stunned. I anointed her with oil that morning and prayed over her. She was crying, and I was crying. I held and comforted her. Right then and there, I felt a sense of peace and hope in knowing that God was continually watching over Jo-An and me and that He had promised never to leave or forsake us. Jo-An got dressed, and we left for the appointment at the school.

At another interview north of Boston, the social worker and one teacher met with Carl and me, while Jo-An sat in on various classes for observation. We filled out an application, took a tour of the school, and met with the school's psychologist three days later. Jo-An was accepted and attended the program from 2003 to 2005. Jo-An was in a healthy, positive, nurturing environment with supportive staff. We could not believe that there were good people left in the world, people who were willing to help us with our daughter.

Notwithstanding, there continued to be challenging days ahead: getting Jo-An dressed in the mornings, getting her to the table on time for breakfast, preparing her lunch, and getting her to the waiting bus. Some days she boarded the bus; at other times, she did not. Every day was different.

By the middle of March, 2003, I had returned to work halftime and was getting full support from my husband, our two sons, and our older daughter. I was attending seminary classes twice per week, at night, and although it was tiring to think of going to seminary classes after working for an entire day, once I got there, the atmosphere of prayer at the beginning of every class would set the tone for the lively presentations and student interaction and support that I gladly received and welcomed. While I was enduring trials, God was doing a new thing by opening doors for me to attend seminary.

As I reminisce, my greatest challenges were when I took Jo-An to her medical and dental appointments and had to wait in the waiting area. My worst nightmare was that she might get agitated, talk loudly, or throw a magazine on the floor, and then all eyes would be on us. I had difficulty at dental appointments where Jo-An refused to allow her dentist to do the work. On another occasion, she did not allow a technician to take an ultrasound or an x-ray. Those kinds of incidents, and more, have occurred many times over. I lived through scores of embarrassing scenes, but it never changed my mission to bring Jo-An out in public. For extra-curricular activities, I tried swimming classes, where Jo-An was excited for two or three classes, then that cycle ended. She had an interview for singing, but she ended up dancing to the sound of the tape that we had brought.

Jo-An has come a long way. She celebrated her twenty-fifth birthday at home with family and friends and had a joyous time. She cried when her childhood friend had to leave. She still has retained a wide vocabulary and reads books and magazines. In 2007, we transferred her medical care nearer to home so she could become familiar with her community.

Twelve years have passed since the start of Jo-An's illness. Jo-An has continued to make slow and steady progress. She is surrounded by a network of people: an occupational therapist who provides in-home therapy once a week, a personal care attendant who comes ten hours a week to help her with personal care, a bus monitor and a driver who provide her with loving care on her daily trips to her program, and her family members who assist daily in coordinating her total care. Through the efforts of a prior counselor, we engaged a group of consultants to provide testing and to suggest new learning styles that would benefit Jo-An. They provided us with a report listing day treatment options that Jo-An's current occupational therapist used to research a suitable day program for her.

Jo-An was accepted to a program on June 23, 2008. Already, she has begun to receive the proper intervention that will help her relearn the tools she had lost. I thank God for allowing me to have some time during the day, to read, write, and utilize my time—God's time, more effectively.

God had been continually at work in Jo-An's life, but we just couldn't see it. We wanted immediate results and could not fathom the depth of God's workmanship. We will never understand why Jo-An suffers mentally or what is God's will for her life, but we know that God loves Jo-An, has created her in His own image and likeness, and has a perfect plan for her life as well as ours. God will unveil His plan for Jo-An when we wait patiently for it.

Prayer:

Father God, Maker of Heaven and Earth
And all that is in it,[1]
I confess my impatience and my frustration.
I repent of these sins and ask for Your forgiveness.
Thank You, Lord,
For keeping me under the umbrella
Of Your wings.[2]

I come to You,
Because there is no one who
Can lighten my darkness;[3]
There is no one, but You, who can provide
Me with the strength I need[4]
To live from day to day.
I look to You, and You alone,
For answers.
Now, Lord, I pray
That You would sustain me.
In Jesus' name, Amen.

The Lord's reply:

"I will never leave you nor forsake you.[5]
I will instruct you and teach you in the way
you should go.[6]
I have loved you with an everlasting love.[7]
You called in trouble, and I
delivered you;
I answered you in the secret
place of thunder."[8]

Reflection:

As I reflected on the years since 1995 and the trials that I have experienced, I realized that I was looking for God to respond positively to all of the issues that I faced. In some instances, He did. However, I failed to see God as a big God whether He chose to answer my prayers or not. God was using that period of time to draw me closer to Him and to mold and fashion me into the woman He has called me to be, for His glory.

Your reflection:

Reflect on the most difficult situation you have ever experienced or are currently experiencing. How are you handling your situation? What is God showing and teaching you?

31

Depending Totally on God

Since 1990, I had been telling God all my problems, angered at how long I had to wait on Him, angry at the situation I was in, doing everything, but realizing that it was time to wait. It was time to change my ways.

In the spring of 1999, I enrolled at a local seminary taking my first class in Church Management. Carl supported me in that effort, caring for Jo-An while I attended classes. The class taught me all aspects of church management, from organizing Bible studies to writing church newsletters. I was always interested in writing when I was a teenager, so the idea of creating a newsletter was fascinating to me. God was giving me the signal to move without doubt. I proceeded to produce my first issue, which was published in the fall of 1999.

In the summer of 1999, during my personal retreat on the Cape, I was praying for family needs. Two months later, in November of 1999, Jo-An was being transferred to another hospital, so I was experiencing more trials. During this period, I listened to the voice of God and constantly and consistently recorded in my journals a Scripture verse that came to mind at that moment concerning the issue for which I was praying. God repeatedly showed me that He was my Shepherd (Psalm 23), that He would deliver me from my fears (Ps.34:4), and that His word would not go void (Is.55:11). I could count on God to come through for me when no one else would. God knew the inside scoop of my life, the difficulties I was encountering. I was trapped in my own prison of hopelessness, praying and waiting for the Master to open the prison gate.

My life continued to move in a downhill and, sometimes, in an uphill spiral. Some days seemed to pass me by without my completing a task. I prayed but did not always get a chance to read my Bible. I was forever cleaning and cooking. It seemed that I was in a constant battle for survival, but God was with me. One day in November, I poured my heart out to God. I cried, because I knew He had kept me from the pangs of death in years past by healing my illnesses and that He had promised to do it again.

In the midst of my hardship, caring for Jo-An, and having the load of running the house, I was excited about classes, the people with whom I was meeting, and the research papers that I was writing. I was stretched to the maximum with seminary studies. By December 4, 2001, I felt like giving up, but God answered my prayer. I wrote these words in my journal:

I have heard all your cries.
Don't you know that I love you
With an everlasting love?[1]
I will make a way for you;[2]
I am the Lord[3] and in an
Acceptable time I will heal

Your land.
All I want from you are your
Praises.
I want you to be saturated in my love
And nurtured at my bosom.
You will want nothing more
But to be focused on my love.
You will never feel insecure,
For my love satisfies all your
Needs and wants.[4]
Do not be anxious about your life
At this time.
I am the Lord; I change not.[5]
I am turning things around for
Your good.
Stand firm on my promises.
I will not let you down.
I am a faithful God.[6]

God continued to move me to the next level and gave me strength to persevere through the storms. I thanked God for allowing me to have a husband who is a great provider and who supported me as I moved forward.

I continued to depend on God for my every need, reminding Him of His promises to heal our daughter Jo-An. In December, 2001, I was ready to consecrate my life to God. I asked Him to change me, and use me. I admitted I was willing to please Him for the rest of my life. I was willing to receive His courage and strength, and to give love to His people. I asked God to take away my weaknesses and allow His grace to be sufficient for me. I realized that I was privileged to receive the seconds, minutes, hours, days, weeks, months, and years that God had given me and that I was not thanking Him enough for what He had done and continued to do for me. I was complaining. I refused to wait. I wanted answers quickly. But who am I? I am a child of God. God is God, and He will always be in control.

Yes, God was in charge of my life and was leading me, although I could not see it physically. He continued to bring Scriptures to my heart after my daily prayers. By the middle of December, 2001, I noted good things happening in my household. Jo-An cried out one day and said, "Lord, have mercy." My job had approved another year of family medical leave for me. I had experienced God's love in the midst of the battle that was raging in my life. I really believed that things did not happen by chance and that Jo-An's situation had taught me to look at life differently.

I was returning from doing some errands on Thursday, September 9, 2004, when my life changed for the worse. I was happy that I had purchased cable and Internet services. I was reviewing the cable on the outside of the house. As I left the car, the car began to roll down the driveway toward another car which was parked across the street. I tried to stop it and landed on my face, with my knees badly damaged. The car hit one parked car, and luckily, no one was hurt. Two people drove slowly as they saw what was happening, got out of their cars, and went to get me some help.

With blood gushing from my knees, and in excruciating pain, I stood up, relieved that my face was not torn, walked inside, and changed my clothes. Within five minutes, the police had come to my assistance, had taken a report, and had called an ambulance to take me to a nearby hospital.

The night seemed long as I went through various tests to check for broken bones and fractures. Next came the cleaning and stitching of the deeper wounds. Ouch! That was painful! It hurt badly, even when I was given pain relievers. I was allergic to morphine and vomited excessively. Monique was there at my side and stayed with me until I was ready to go home. Carl stayed at home with Jo-An.

Monique came by that Friday and the week following to help get Jo-An on the bus. She brought me food that Saturday afternoon. Carl was also very helpful in the mornings before he left for work. In the days and weeks following, I suffered with pain: it was painful getting off my bed, walking downstairs, going outside, and standing at the bottom of the driveway to get Jo-An off the bus in the afternoons. I felt lonely lying on the bed from day to day, having to help myself and Jo-An, who relied on me totally. It was quite difficult!

As I later reviewed the events of that week, I began to thank God for His mighty hands upon my life. I thanked Him for His greatness, His loving kindness, and His mercy toward me.[7] His hands of mercy had pulled me up from the ground and allowed me to walk into our home to change my clothes. God had sent strangers to assist in getting an ambulance to take me to the hospital. He had sent doctors and nurses to help me throughout the night. I was thankful to God for my husband Carl and for our daughter Monique. God had sent the Holy Spirit to comfort me through the pain and the difficult nights that I experienced. The Lord had used this time to give me a chance to rest, pray, and seek Him.

God showed me how much He loved me and how He had forgiven me of all my sins. He assured me that He was in the business of restoring

His servants to wholeness, and that He is a God of second chances.

Prayer:

Sweet, sweet, Jesus and God my Father,[8]
I adore You and magnify Your Name this day,
My God, my Savior[9] and my Redeemer.[10]
I confess, Lord, that I have taken You for granted.
I repent of this sin and ask for Your forgiveness.
Thank You for protecting me,[11]
Comforting me,[12] and giving me hope.[13]
I pray that You would give me another chance
To totally depend on You.
In Jesus' name, Amen.

The Lord's reply:

"Wait for the Lord;
be strong and take heart
and wait for the Lord."[14]

Reflection:

God is my joy[15] in the midst of sorrows.
He is my peace[16] in the midst of a storm.
He is my strength[17] when I am weak.
He is my hope[18] in the midst of despair.

He is love[19] when I am experiencing hate.
God is the One Who made my way perfect.[20]
God is the One Who was guiding me.[21]

Your reflection:

Reflect now, on the struggles that you are going through or have gone through. The time is always right to depend fully on God, by relinquishing your burdens to Him. He will make a way out of the struggles you face.

32

Growing in Faith

If anyone had asked me twelve or more years ago what I would have done about my situation, it would definitely not be the same answer that I would give today. My situation has changed a little, but the major changes have come from within my heart. God continues to work in me.

Years ago, I was not totally dependent on God and was operating on my own strength. That brought on tiredness, doubts, and fears. When I turned to trusting God about Jo-An, and took little steps getting help with her care, God gave me the strength to take bigger ones. Also, when I viewed Jo-An's situation differently, as a gift and not as a burden, things took a different turn. Granted, each day was different. Some days I would talk about my troubles; other days I would not. However, I began to yield to God's plans and wishes to love and help Jo-An because she was one of His chosen daughters.

Every day I would wake up, I would thank God for giving me life. God has sent some help my way, but the bulk of the responsibility still rests on Carl and me as parents.

In the meantime, I am concentrating on knowing my purpose and helping others. I understand now, that over the past years God was guiding, upholding, and giving me strength through His Word, which was all I could depend on. No one understood my pain, my suffering, or my frustration. God did. He was molding and shaping me into the person He wanted me to be, loving, kind, faithful, and compassionate to others. He was establishing me, building my character, giving me wisdom and patience, healing my fears and my brokenness, bringing me closer to Him, and showing me that my focus was to be on Him, not on my problems. Most of all, He wanted me to live a life of faith and trust in Him.

I am growing in faith because God is in control of my life, helping me every step of the way. He has taught me through trials and waits to see if I will pass every test, so I can be elevated to the next level. Because of this, I refuse to bathe myself in self-defeat or self-pity. I have decided to take this faith-walk regardless of my circumstances; this faith-walk is based on a relationship between God and me. I have purposed to take God at His word and invest my time living a life of faith and resting in God's everlasting arms.

Prayer:

I will extol You, my God, O King;
I will bless Your name forever and ever.
Every day I will bless You
And I will praise Your Name

Forever and ever.[1]
Thank You for Your love,[2] patience,[3] and
Faithfulness[4] toward me.
Lord, I pray that, by faith,
I would see what You are
Doing; and would
Stand on Your promises
Regardless of the situation I face
Or how I feel.
I also pray that the light and joy
Of Jesus would radiate in my life
As well as in others.
In Jesus' name, Amen.

The Lord's reply:

"Put on the whole armor of God, that you may be able to stand against the wiles of the devil. For we do not wrestle against flesh and blood, but against principalities, against powers, against the rulers of the darkness of this age, against spiritual hosts of wickedness in the heavenly places. Therefore take up the whole armor of God, that you may be able to withstand in the evil day, and having done all, to stand."[5]

Reflection:

What we see with our naked eye does not count. What counts is what we hope for and in whom we believe. Our faith is what God uses to bless us. If we believe that Jesus died and rose again and that all things are in His hands, then we can put our hope in Him by standing on His promises, utilizing prayer, and having faith in the One who has secured for us salvation and eternal life.

Your reflection:

Reflect on a difficult time that you are experiencing or have experienced in your life. Pray and release that difficulty to God. Rejoice and believe you have received your change by faith although you have not seen it. Reflect on how God has helped you in the past. What have you learned from your prior experiences? Write your reflections here.

Endnotes

Chapter 1

[1] "Trinidad and Tobago," *Wikipedia, the Free Encyclopedia.* Http://en.wikipedia.org/wiki/Trinidad_and_Tobago (Accessed July, 2008).

[2] Ibid.

[3] Ibid.

[4] Ibid.

[5] Ibid.

[6] Ibid.

[7] Ps. 121:2

[8] Ps. 50:1-2

[9] Rev. 3:8

Chapter 2

[1] Is. 41:10

[2] Ps. 32:8

[3] Ps. 28:7

[4] Ps.71:5

[5] 1 Pet. 5:7

Chapter 3

[1] 2 Chr. 1:10

[2] Heb. 12:2

[3] Matt. 6:8

[4] Ps. 37:3, 4

[5] Matt. 6:8

Chapter 4

[1] Rev. 19:6

[2] Phil. 2:9

[3] Deut. 3:24

[4] Zech. 4:6

Chapter 5

[1] Is. 6:3

[2] Gal. 2:20

[3] John 3:16

[4] Ps. 65:2

Chapter 6

[1] Ps. 40:17

[2] Ps. 29:11

[3] Prov. 22:6

Chapter 7

[1] Ps. 118:24 NKJV

[2] Ps. 46:1

[3] 1 Pet. 5:7

[4] Phil. 4:19

[5] Ps. 84:11

Chapter 8

[1] Rev. 4:2

[2] Ps. 32:8

[3] Ps. 37:23

Chapter 9

[1] Ps. 150:6 NKJV

[2] Ps. 105:1-3

Chapter 10

[1] Is. 9:6

[2] Rom. 8:28

[3] Is. 43:3; Ps. 71:5

[4] Luke 12:22, 23

[5] Luke 12:30, 31

Chapter 11

[1] Ps. 69:30 NKJV

[2] Ps. 126:3

[3] Is. 46:11

[4] Prov. 18:22

Chapter 12

[1] Ps. 24:5

[2] Ps. 46:11

[3] Jer. 31:3 NKJV [him] Added by Author

Chapter 13

[1] Ps. 63:3

[2] Ps. 139:7-8

[3] Ps. 139:2

[4] Is. 51:12-13

[5] Rom. 8:28

[6] 1 Thess.5:18

Chapter 14

[1] Is. 9:6

[2] Rev. 3:20

[3] Matt. 11:28-30

Chapter 15

[1] Ps. 71:5

[2] Ps. 18:2

[3] Ps. 28:6

[4] Phil. 4:6,7

Chapter 16

[1] Rev. 19:16

[2] Ps. 40:16

[3] Jer. 31:33

[4] Ps. 139:7-10

[5] Is. 43:1-2

Chapter 17

[1] Num. 14:18. NKJV Ps. 24:8

[2] Ex. 3:14

[3] 1 John 4:19

[4] Rom. 5:8

[5] 1 John 4:18 NKJV

Chapter 18

[1] Is. 51:15

[2] Is. 41:8

[3] John 15:12-13 NKJV

Chapter 19

[1] See the following Bible passages: (Is.9:6; John 10:9; Jos.1:5; Phil.4:19; Rom.8:28; Rom.16:27; Ps.92:2; Ps.103:3,4).

[2] Ps. 115:15

[3] Ps. 33:1

[4] Eph. 2:4; Jer. 31:3

[5] Eph. 4:31, 32

Chapter 20

[1] 1 Pet. 2:21

[2] Gal. 5:1 [you] Added by Author.

Chapter 21

[1] Ps. 24:8

[2] Acts 7:49

[3] Phil. 2:13

[4] Matt. 6:14-15

Chapter 22

[1] James F. Balch, and Phyllis A Balch, *Prescription for Nutritional Healing* (New York: Avery Publishing Group, 1997), 3.

[2] Ibid.

[3] Ibid.

[4] Ibid., p.4.

[5] Ibid., p. 5.

[6] Ibid.

[7] Ibid.

[8] John Messmer, *The Benefits of Antioxidants*, The Diet Channel, March 2007. <Http://www.thedietchannel.com/The-Benefits-of-Antioxidants> (Accessed July, 2008).

[9] 1 Pet.1:16

[10] 2 Cor. 1:3

[11] 1 Cor. 6:19-20

Chapter 23

[1] Ps. 19:1 NKJV

[2] Ps. 91:16

[3] Ps. 68:5 NASB

Chapter 24

[1] 1 John 4:19

[2] Rev. 4:11

[3] 2 Cor. 1:2

[4] 1 John 4:19

[5] Ps. 121:5

[6] Is. 42:16

[7] Rom. 15:5

[8] Is. 40:31

Chapter 25

[1] 1 Chr. 29:13

[2] Phil. 2:9-10

[3] Col. 2:13-15

[4] Neh. 8:10

[5] John 14:27

[6] Neh. 8:10

Chapter 26

[1] Ps. 24:8

[2] 2 Chr. 7:14

Chapter 27

[1] Rev. 5:12

[2] Deut. 5:16

Chapter 28

[1] Ps. 28:7

[2] Ps. 139:7-10

[3] Deut. 31:6

[4] Ps. 46:1

[5] 2 Cor. 12:9

Chapter 29

[1] Ps. 24:8

[2] Ps. 46:1

[3] Matt. 17:20

[4] Heb. 11:6

Chapter 30

[1] Heb. 1:10

[2] Ps. 36:7

[3] 1 Pet. 2:9

[4] 2 Cor. 12:9

[5] Deut. 31:8; Jos. 1:5

[6] Ps. 32:8

[7] Jer. 31:3

[8] Ps. 81:7 NKJV

Chapter 31

[1] Jer.31:3

[2] Is.43:16

[3] Is.42:6

[4] 1John 4:18

[5] Mal.3:6 KJV

[6] Deut. 7:9

[7] See the following Bible passages: (Ps.48:1; Ps. 103:4; Ps.119:132).

[8] 2 Thess. 1:1

[9] Is. 43:3

[10] Is. 43:14

[11] Ps. 46:1

[12] 2 Cor. 1:3

[13] 1 Tim. 1:1

[14] Ps. 27:14

[15] Ps. 43:4

[16] Eph. 2:14

[17] Ps. 28:8

[18] 1 Tim. 1:1

[19] 1 John 4:8

[20] Is. 43:16

[21] Ps. 32:8

Chapter 32

[1] Ps. 145:1-2 NKJV

[2] Eph. 2:4

[3] Rom. 15:5

[4] Ps. 119:90

[5] Eph. 6:11-13 NKJV

Bibliography

Balch, James, F. and Phyllis A. Balch. *Prescription for Nutritional Healing.* New York: Avery Publishing Group, 1997.

Messmer, John, *The Benefits of Antioxidants*. The Diet Channel. <Http://www.thedietchannel.com/The-Benefits-of-Antioxidants> (Accessed July, 2008).

"Trinidad and Tobago." *Wikipedia, The Free Encyclopedia.* <Http://en.wikipedia.org/wiki/Trinidad_and_Tobago> (Accessed July, 2008).